Take me home, I'm yo

D1354047

# The (Secret) Toy Society

## WHAT YOU'LL NEED

*Pattern (page 207)*

*Main fabric,
18 inches (24 centimeters)
by 22 inches (56 centimeters)*

*Contrasting fabric,
8 inches (20 centimeters)
square for inside of the ears,
muzzle, and belly*

*Stuffing*

*Felt and embroidery thread
for facial details*

*Scissors*

*Pins*

*Needle and thread*

The (Secret) Toy Society is a worldwide guerrilla kindness project. It consists of toy makers—of all skill levels—who make toys and leave them in public as gifts to be found by passersby. The project was begun in 2008 by an Australian crafter as an attempt to create a "something for nothing" experience. Since then, the society has attracted over 3,200 members around the world and has so far gifted an estimated 1,800 toys.

For my version of this project, I've created an animal doll that can be customized in any number of ways. Here I've made a tiger by using orange and black striped fabric and a contrasting fabric of orange with stars. However, check the list further down the page for other animals you can make with the same pattern.

To make the eyes and other facial details, use felt and/or embroidery. Note that buttons can be a choking hazard for younger kids, and you never know who is going to find it.

## DIRECTIONS

1. Photocopy pattern and cut out each shape you're going to use.

2. Pin arm to contrasting fabric and cut 4.

3. Place two arms with the right sides together and stitch around, leaving shoulder end open. Repeat for other arm.

4. Pin leg to contrasting fabric and cut 4.

5. Place two legs with the right sides together and stitch around, leaving hip end open. Repeat for other leg.

6. Pin ear to contrasting fabric and cut 2; pin ear to main fabric and cut 2.

7. Place a contrasting fabric ear and a main fabric ear

with the right sides together and stitch around, leaving the base of the ear closest to the head open. Repeat for other ear.

8. Snip the curve of each of the ends of the limbs and ears (see page 178 for snipping curves).

9. Turn the arms, legs, and ears right side out. If you're having trouble turning the little limbs, you can insert the rounded end of a knitting needle or pencil into the limb and gently push the ends out.

10. Stuff the limbs.

11. Lay one body right side up and position the limbs as shown.

12. Place the other body right side down and pin together.

13. Stitch carefully around the body. If you're using a sewing machine, sew slowly over the limbs. Leave a gap for turning as shown on the pattern.

14. Turn right side out. The trick to turning this little toy right side out is pulling its limbs out first.

15. Stuff the toy and stitch the gap closed (don't forget to fold the hem allowance in). Remember to stitch it firmly as kids can be rough on their toys.

16. If you're using a tail, cut, sew, turn, and stuff the tail as you did with the limbs. Tuck the raw ends of the tail in and whip stitch the tail shut. Then you can position it on the little animal's rear end, pin it in place and hand stitch it on.

17. Cut the muzzle out and snip around on the grey snip lines to create the hem allowance.

18. Position the muzzle on the face and pin into place.

19. Tuck the snipped hem under and whip stitch the muzzle onto the face. You can tuck as you go if you like as it can be tricky to capture every little bit under a pin.

20. If you're using it, the belly is sewn the same way as the muzzle.

21. Cut out the eyes and stitch the black circle one the white. Try to position the black circle in the middle of the white so the toy will be looking straight out at its new owner.

22. Position eyes and nose on the face. Move them around until you're happy and then pin them in place.

23. Whip stitch them on.

24. You can use embroidery thread for other details such as whiskers or the anchor-shaped cat's mouth.

## OTHER ANIMALS TO MAKE

Use yellow fabric and pointed ears for a lion. You can make the mane by snipping about 45 pieces of 5-inch (12½ centimeters) lengths of ribbon, folding them in half, and placing them under the ears (with folds facing towards the nose) when you're pinning the head together. For this lion I also used a little more of the contrasting fabric for the paws.

✦ Brown fabric and the round ears make a monkey.

✦ Ginger or black fabric and the pointed ears make a cat.

- Black and white fabric and round ears make a panda.

- Grey fabric, a wide smile, and downward sloping dark shapes around the eyes make a sloth.

- Brown fabric, the rounded ears, and making the limbs wider by ½ inch (2 centimeters) on all sides make a bear; the same choices but white fabric for a polar bear (bears also have a little stubby tail, so you can shorten the tail or just not use it).

- Grey fabric, the rounded ears (white on the inside, grey on the outside), and making shorter, wider limbs make a koala.

To distribute the toys, put each new friend in a clear ziplock bag (to keep it from getting dirty or wet and to show the finder that it's clean and has been placed with care). Attach a tag that reads "Take me I'm yours" (or words to that effect) in the bag so it's clearly visible. You can include a hashtag (#thetoysociety, #thesecrettoysociety, #guerrillakindness, or #randomactsofkindness) and/or your social media handle on the back of the tag so people can find out more about the project, or you can leave it anonymous if you prefer. Then drop the toy somewhere it will be found, such as a playground, picnic area, library, or medical center, or other places families visit.

thetoysociety.blogspot.com / www.facebook.com/TheSecretToySociety

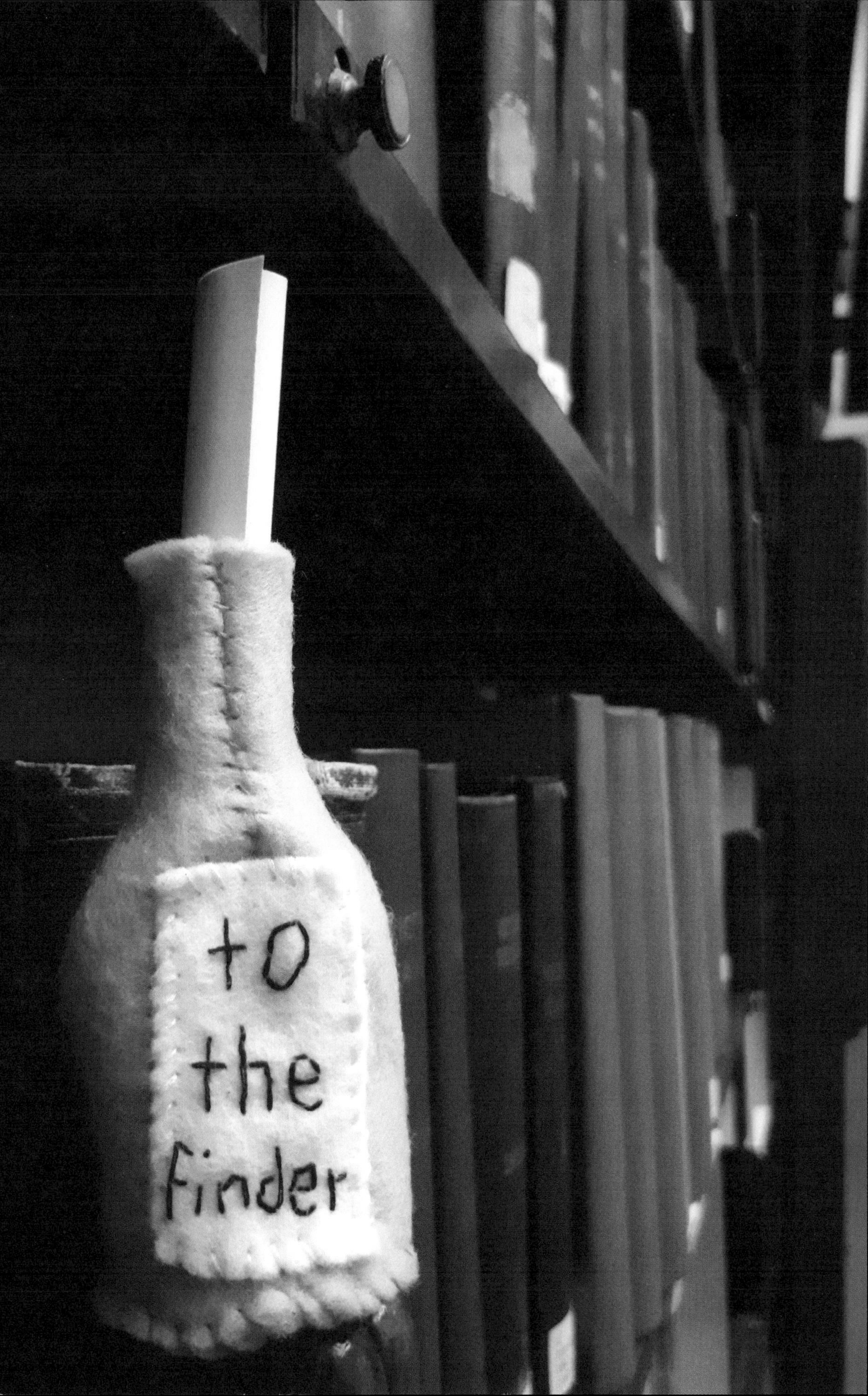
to
the
finder

# Message in a Bottle

*Pattern (page 208)*

*Felt for bottle[1]*

*Felt or cotton fabric for label*

*Scissors*

*Pins*

*Needle and thread*

*Piece of paper 4½ inches (12 centimeters) by 3 inches (8 centimeters) for the message*

This project is super quick and playful. It's a great one to drop in libraries, museums, or other inside spaces.

## DIRECTIONS

1. Pin your paper pattern to your felt and cut out. You'll need four of the bottle pieces and one each of the bottom and label pieces.

2. Place two bottle sides together and stitch along the edge, leaving the neck and base open. Repeat for other 3 side seams.

3. Turn the felt bottle inside out.

1 I like to stick to glass colors; pale green and blue works best, but you can go with any color you like.

4. Stitch bottle base in place. A good technique is to place the base inside the bottle body, matching the edges to each other, and pinch them together. Stitch and then rotate the bottle around, pinching together again. Repeat until whole base stitched into the bottle body.

5. Freehand stitch "To the finder" or something similar on the label. It's small, so I'd use sewing thread rather than embroidery thread. If you're not confident about freehand stitching, you can also write on a label made from cotton fabric.

6. Stitch the label to the side of the bottle.

7. Run the end of a pen or knitting needle down the seams from inside the bottle to pop them out.

8. For the paper message, write something lovely on your piece of paper and roll it up tightly. Tie some thread around it to keep it rolled and put it in the bottle. I like to make sure the paper roll is thinner than the bottle neck so it can lean to one side in the bottle rather than fill the bottle neck up.

9. Place it somewhere for someone to find. If it's gotten a little squished before you put it out, simply take the roll of paper out and run the end of the pen or knitting needle down the seams once more before "dropping'" it somewhere for a stranger.

# CHAPTER TWO

# Knitting and Crochet

~~~~~~~~~~~~~~~~~~~

When knitting these type of projects, I like to use sports weight (8 ply) yarn and US 1.5/metric 2.5 mm/UK 12 or 13 size needles. The bigger your needles, the bigger the holes between stitches, and the more stuffing you can see through the knitting. The same goes for yarn; the thinner the yarn, the bigger the holes in the knitting. So I like to use thin needles and regular thickness yarn to get the best mix and not see the stuffing.

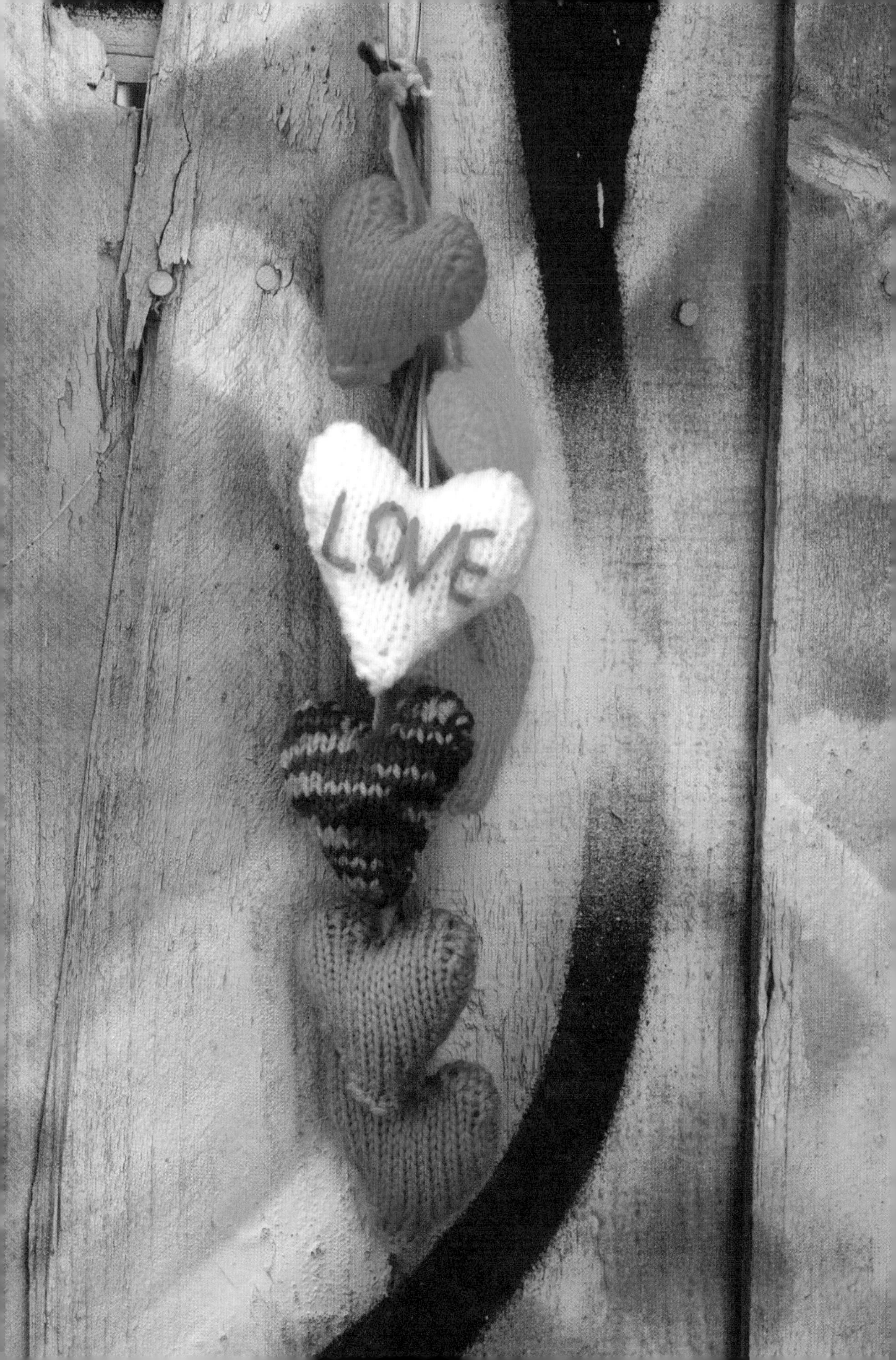
LOVE

# Knitted Heart

*Knitting needles (US 2/
metric 2.5 mm/UK 12)*

*Row counter*

*Yarn—sports weight (8 ply)
26 feet (800 centimeters)*

*Darning or yarn needle*

*Scissors*

*Stuffing*

Sometimes your activism is going to need a little heart. It might become part of a yarn bomb, it might be a guerrilla kindness piece, it might be a gift for someone who needs it, or it might be part of a barter. You can string five or six hearts along a ribbon to make bunting, or you might attach a safety pin to the back of one to make it a brooch. However you choose to use them, they're quick to knit up and easy to customize with colors and slogans. I've stitched the word "love" with yarn using a simple backstitch (see the backstitch instructions on page 191 if you're in need of a little help).

These hearts are knitted in stocking stitch.

## DIRECTIONS

✦ Cast on 4 stitches.

* Row 1: Knit

* Row 2: Increase at start of row, knit to end of row

* Row 3 and 4: Repeat row 2 (7 stitches)

✦ Leave these stitches on the needle and cut your yarn, leaving a long tail to weave in later. Then cast on another 4 stitches onto the same needle and repeat these instructions again to knit the second little curve to create the top of your heart.

* Row 5: Knit across all stitches (14 stitches).

* Row 6 to 10: Knit.

* Row 11: Decrease at start of row,
  knit to end of row.

* Repeat row 11, 9 times more (4 stitches).

* Row 21: Cast off.

**TO MAKE UP**

Knit two hearts. Place the two hearts with right sides together. Start stitching from the point of the heart, up the side, around the curves and halfway down the other side.

Turn right side out, stuff, and whipstitch closed. If it looks a little lopsided once you've finished it, squish the heart around in your fingers to shape it properly.

You can stitch a loop at the top of the heart for hanging.

If the colors you want to use don't divide nicely into the 20 rows of the heart, it's easy to modify the pattern. For example, I wanted to knit the queer flag, and there are 6 colors that needed to be fit in. Between the curves of the heart where you're increasing and the last 10 rows where you're decreasing, you can add or subtract as many rows as you need. The little queer heart has 24 rows instead of the regular 21.

## The Queer Flag

In 1977, American gay activist Gilbert Baker was challenged by Harvey Milk, an American gay activist, movement leader, and politician, to come up with a symbol of pride for the gay community. In response to this challenge, Baker sewed the first rainbow flag, which included a hot pink stripe at the top. He assigned meanings to the colors: hot pink = sex, red = life, orange = healing, yellow = sunlight, green = nature, turquoise = magic/art, indigo = serenity, and violet = spirit. The flag has been revised several times and is now usually accepted as having only six colors; the indigo and turquoise have been changed to a royal blue, although there are many variants, including one with black and brown stripes at the top to represent people of color.

Darling, I want
my gay rights
NOW

STONEWALL

# Knitted Protest Dolls

*Knitting needles
(US 2/metric 2.5 mm/UK 12)*

*Yarn—sports weight (8 ply) in:*

*Teal blue, 135 feet
(4100 centimeters)*

*Mid-brown, 15 feet
(500 centimeters)*

*Dark brown, 21½ feet
(660 centimeters)*

*Lavender, 10 feet
(300 centimeters)*

*Darning or yarn needle*

*Stuffing*

*Row counter*

*Felt in white, black,
and teal blue*

*Thin cardboard
(I used a cereal box)*

*Toothpick*

*Carpenters/white/PVA
(polyvinyl acetate)
glue or hot glue*

*Permanent marker*

*Scissors*

*Needle and thread*

**Optional**

*Pearls*

There are many inspirational people in the world, and sometimes it's nice to make tiny versions of then to keep around and inspire you daily. They also make great guerrilla kindness drops and can be prominently installed in public spaces with special relevance to the inspiring people themselves.

Here I've knitted three inspirational women: Marsha P. Johnson, Julia Gillard, and a member of Pussy Riot.

This doll is super simple to knit and easily customizable with pants, long or short dress, and skirt options. Each doll is knitted from the toes up using in stocking stitch. If you don't know how to knit, it's all explained starting on page 179. To change colors in the middle of knitting a row seems tricky, but it's really not. There are instructions for that on page 183.

Here I've provided the pattern for Marsha. If you want to design your own protest doll, head down to the second set of instructions to create anyone you wish.

## DIRECTIONS

### FEET (KNIT 2)

Cast on 12 stitches in lavender

Row 1 to 7: knit

Cast off

### LONG DRESS (KNIT 2)

Cast on 22 stitches in teal

Row 1: knit

Row 2 to 11: Decrease at start, knit to end of row

Row 12 to 65: knit

CAST OFF

### ARMS (KNIT 2)

Cast on 8 stitches in mid-brown

Row 1 to 5: knit

Row 6 to 30: change to teal, knit to end of row

Cast off

### BACK OF HEAD (KNIT 1)

Cast on 10 stitches in dark brown

Row 1 to 3: knit

Row 4 to 5: Increase at start and end of row

Row 6 to 18: knit

Row 19 to 21: Decrease at start and end of row

Cast off

### FRONT OF HEAD AND FACE (KNIT 1)

Cast on 10 stitches in mid-brown

Row 1 to 3: knit

Row 4 to 5: Increase at start and end of row

Row 6 to 9: knit

Row 10: knit 1 dark brown, 10 mid-brown, 1 dark brown

Row 11: knit 2 dark brown, 8 mid-brown, 2 dark brown

Row 12 to 17: knit 3 dark brown, 6 mid-brown, 3 dark brown

Row 18: knit dark brown

Row 19 to 21: Decrease at start and end of row in dark brown

Cast off

## DRESS RUFFLE (KNIT 1)

Cast on 60 stitches

Row 1 to Row 3: knit

Cast off

## TO MAKE UP

The body and head are sewn up wrong sides together and then turned right side out. The arms and legs (or feet) are sewn up wrong sides together.

## LEGS/FEET AND ARMS

Fold the arm, leg, or foot in half with the wrong sides together and whipstitch the long open end. When sewing up the open hole at the ends of the hands and feet, I find it helpful to picture the hole as a clock face. Sew from 12 o'clock to 6 o'clock and pull closed, then take the needle from 3 o'clock to 9 o'clock and pull closed. Two more stitches—2 to 7 and 10 to 4—should close the end of the limb up. However, feel free to run a couple more stitches across the limb end if you feel it's looking a little lumpy.

## BODY/DRESS

When sewing up the body or dress, place the two dress pieces right sides together and sew from the shoulder down the side, across the bottom, and up the other side, leaving the top open to turn through. This makes it easier to stuff the corners at the bottom of the dress.

## HEAD

Place the front and back of the head with the right sides together and stitch from the corner of the neck up and across the head and back down again. Leave the neck open for turning and stuffing.

## STUFFING THE DOLL

When stuffing the doll, especially in the arms and legs, use lots of small pinches of stuffing rather than big handfuls at once. Using large lumps is like stuffing a small stocking with oranges: the stuffing will bunch up and not spread smoothly into all the spaces. Use the rounded end of a knitting needle to push the stuffing into the little limbs.

## SEWING THE FACE

Two small circles of black felt is all you need for the eyes. Move them around on the face until you're happy with the placement and whipstitch on using a needle and thread. I chose not to sew a mouth as I felt their voice was clear through their placards, but feel free to give them a mouth if you prefer. Simply cut a mouth shape out of felt and stitch it on as you did the eyes.

## FINISHING THE DOLL

Once your doll is knitted, sewn, and stuffed, you can continue to customize it with other details.

For example, Marsha P. Johnson got a couple of extra details: flowers and pearls in her hair, a ruffle and sash for her dress, and bright blue eyeshadow.

The flowers are two layers of white felt cut in a little flower shape and secured to her head with a couple of small stitches through the middle of the flower.

I pinned the ruffle to her dress in a wavy line and stitched it down with matching thread.

The sash was a simple circle of purple felt stitched at the back to her dress to hold it on. I freehand stitched the word "Stonewall" into it.

Her eyeshadow was a bright blue oval of felt layered between her eyes and her face.

## FOR THE SIGN

1. Cut a small rectangle out of your cardboard. Measurements will depend entirely on what you want to write on it and how big your writing is.

2. Write your slogan.

3. Turn your little sign over and place the toothpick against it. Make sure the rounder, blunt end is against the sign and the pointier end is hanging over the edge about 2 inches (5 centimeters).

4. Glue the toothpick onto the cardboard.

5. If you've used carpenters, white, or PVA (polyvinyl acetate) glue, leave it for a couple of hours to overnight to dry. Hot glue should be dry in a few minutes.

6. To place the sign on the doll, gently poke it into the hand using a screwing motion to get the toothpick through the knitting and stuffing. Go gently, you don't want to break the toothpick!

7. You can secure the sign into the doll's hand by dipping the toothpick into glue before piercing it through the hand but I find the sign stays nicely in the hand without the need of glue, and that way you can change the protest doll's slogan whenever you like.

## DESIGNING YOUR OWN DOLL

Consider the person you're creating. What are the features that come to mind when you think of them? When you do an image search of them on the internet, what do you notice about them that you want to include in your doll? For example, Julia Gillard has red hair and wears smart suits, so for her distinctive hair style, I knitted her hair straight up and then made a couple of stitches from the middle of her head to the side to create a fringe. Marsha P. Johnson was well known for wearing flowers in her hair, and in one of the most popular photos of her, she has a blue ruffled dress and a purple sash with Stonewall displayed on it. For the Pussy Riot member, I drew my inspiration from the famous photo of them performing in the church. One of them is wearing brown boots, pink tights, a green dress and a yellow balaclava.

You'll find you only need a couple of color and clothing choices to suggest the person.

You'll find the protest doll grid patterns on page 209 for you to fill in with your color choices.

The doll is 72 rows tall from toes to shoulders. You can choose to make a doll with:

- ❑ Shoes and a long dress (feet 7 rows, dress 65 rows)

- ❑ Shoes, legs, and a knee length dress (feet 7 rows, legs 10 rows, dress 55 rows)

- ❑ Shoes, legs, and a short dress (feet 7 rows, legs 23 rows, dress 42 rows)

- ❑ Shoes, legs, a knee length skirt, and a shirt (feet 7 rows, legs 10 rows, skirt 13 rows, shirt 42 rows)

- ❑ Shoes, pants, and a shirt (feet 7 rows, legs 23 rows, shirt 35 rows)

And it's the same with sleeve length. The arm is 30 rows long.

- ❑ Long sleeves (hands 5 rows, sleeve 25 rows)

- ❑ Elbow length sleeves (hands and arms 15 rows, sleeve 15 rows)

- ❑ T-shirt sleeves (hands and arms 25 rows, sleeve 5 rows)

- ❑ No sleeves (arm 30 rows)

Amount of yarn you'll need (these are approximate depending on how tightly you knit):

- ❑ Short dress, 57½ feet (1750 centimeters)

- ❑ Mid-length dress, 70½ feet (2150 centimeters)

- ❑ Long dress, 90 feet (2700 centimeters)

- ❑ Body, 111½ feet (3400 centimeters)

- ❑ Hand/long sleeve, 5½ / 27 feet (160 / 814 centimeters)

- ❑ Hand and arm/elbow sleeve, 10 / 18 feet (300 / 550 centimeters)

- ❑ Hand and arm/T-shirt sleeve, 28 / 5 feet (850 / 150 centimeters)

- ❑ Hand and arm/no sleeve, 38 feet (1150 centimeters)

- ❑ Foot/long pants 5 / 14 feet (150 / 426 centimeters)

- ❑ Foot and leg/mid-length shorts 11 / 9 feet (320 / 247 centimeters)

- ❑ Back of head, 16 feet (487 centimeters)

- ❑ Front of head/hair, 10½ feet / 6½ feet (320 / 200 centimeters)

Plus anything else you want to knit, like Marsha's ruffle.

**Marsha P. Johnson (1945–1992)**

Marsha P. (Pay It No Mind) Johnson was an African American transgender woman. She was an outspoken gay liberation activist, sex worker, and drag queen. Johnson featured prominently in the Stonewall riots which sparked the gay rights movement and the modern fight for LGBTQAI+ rights in America. During one LGBT rally in the early '70s, when asked by a reporter why she was there, she shouted to the microphone, "Darling, I want my gay rights now." Johnson was well known on the streets of New York and often wore elaborate hairstyles which incorporated flowers, pearls, and feathers. There's no website dedicated to her and her work, but a quick internet search will bring up loads of information on this incredible woman.

**Julia Gillard (Born 1961)**

Julia Gillard was Australia's first ever female Prime Minster, leading the country from 2010–2013. She is also the first female to have been the Deputy Prime Minister and the leader of a major Australian political party. During her term as Prime Minister, Gillard was subjected to intense sexism from other members of parliament as well as the media. This culminated in a spontaneous speech in parliament now known as the Misogyny Speech in which she hit back at the Leader of the Opposition's double standards on sexism: "…we are entitled to a better standard than this." The speech is magnificent, do an internet search to read or watch it in full.

**Pussy Riot**

Pussy Riot is a protest punk band from Russia whose lyrics focus on feminism, LGBTQI+ rights, and opposition to Russian President Vladimir Putin. They wear colorful balaclavas to protect their identity during their performances. The band shot to fame around the world when five of their members performed a song called Punk Prayer in a Russian Orthodox Church. Three members were later arrested, and two, Nadia Tolokonnikova and Maria Alyokhina, were jailed for two years.

facebook.com/wearepussyriot

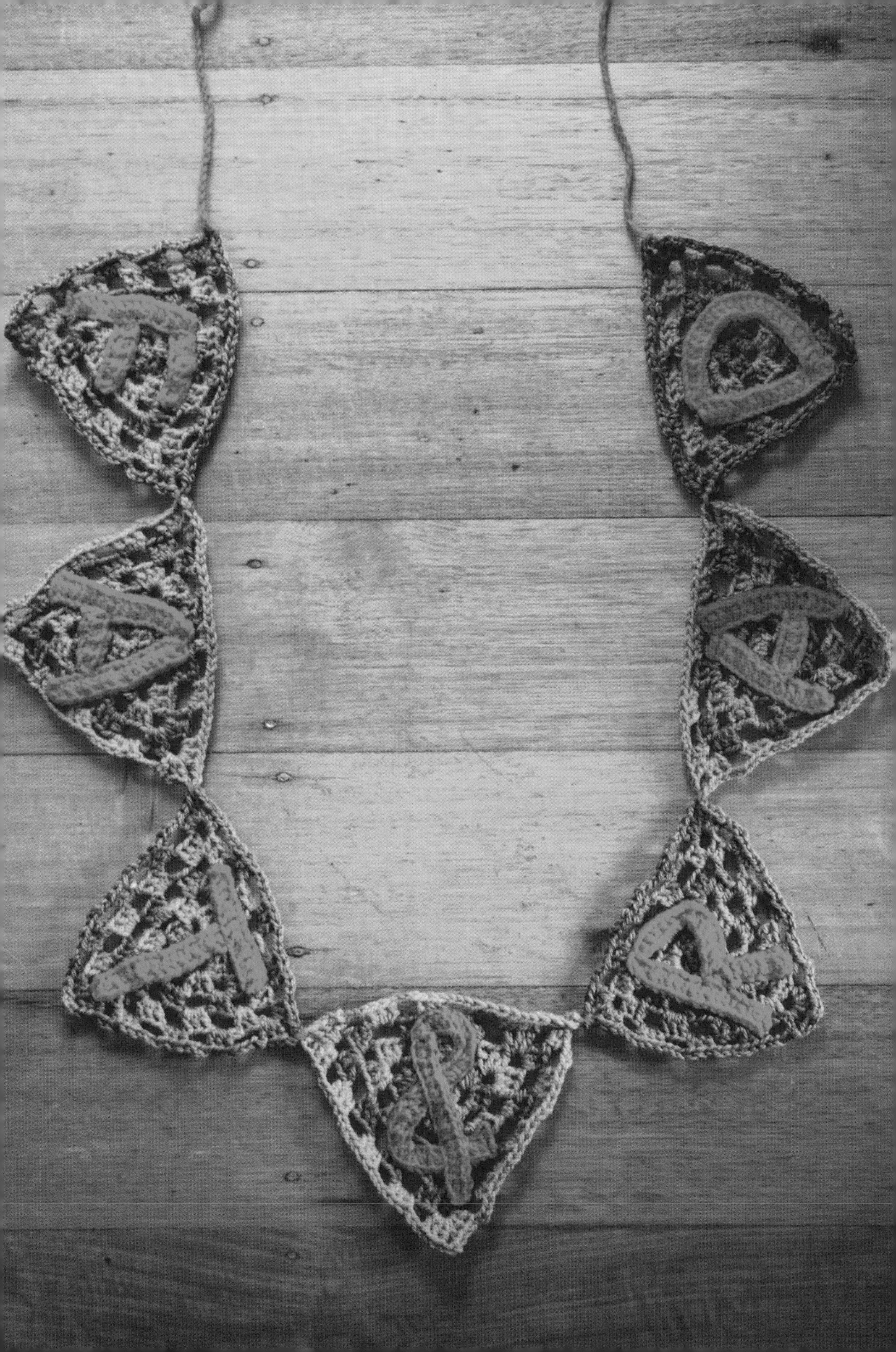

# Crochet Granny Bunting

*Crochet hook*

*Yarn—sports weight (8 ply)*

*Single color flag, 61 feet
(1860 centimeters)*

*Two color flag, 48 feet
(1463 centimeters)
each color*

*The average letter will take
16 feet (487 centimeters)*

*Darning or yarn needle*

*Scissors*

*Needle and thread*

Granny bunting is the triangle version of granny squares, and it's one of the simplest crochet styles to do.

When picking your slogan, a longer slogan might require doing the bunting in several lengths (depending on where you want to install it); i.e., "SMASH THE PATRIARCHY" could be done in two lengths, as "SMASH THE" and "PATRIARCHY" or each word could have its own length.

If you don't know how to crochet, no problem! There are illustrated instructions from page 186 which will show you everything you need to know.

These crochet bunting triangles are made of alternating colors, but feel free to work them in a single color if you prefer. If you do choose to go with a single color, instead of cutting the yarn each time you finish a round, simply slip stitch along the crochet until you get to the next corner and start the new round as instructed.

Crochet Granny Bunting

Slip Stitch
Chain stitch
Double crochet (US)
Treble Crochet (UK)

Letters

*For beginner crocheters, the stitches used in this pattern are:*

chain
slip stitch
double crochet (UK treble crochet)

## DIRECTIONS

To start: chain 5, slip stitch to make a loop

## ROUND 1:

1. Chain 3 (this counts as the first double crochet)

2. Work 2 double crochet

3. Chain 3

4. Work 3 double crochet

5. Chain 3

6. Repeat steps 4 and 5 once more

7. Slip stitch to close the round, pulling the yarn end firmly to make the knot tight

8. Cut your yarn, leaving a tail to weave in later. This should make a tiny triangle with 3 clusters of double crochet and 3 sets of chain with 3 spaces between.

## ROUND 2:

1. Starting at any corner, chain 3

2. Work 2 double crochet

3. Chain 3

4. Work 3 double crochet into the same corner gap as in step 9

5. Chain 3 to the next corner

6. Work 3 double crochet

7. Chain 3

8. Work 3 double crochet into the same corner gap as in step 14

9. Repeat from step 13 once more

10. Chain 3

11. Slip stitch to close the round, pulling the yarn end firmly to make the knot tight.

12. Cut your yarn, leaving a tail to weave in later. This should make a slightly bigger triangle with more pronounced corners.

## ROUND 3:

1. Starting at any corner, chain 3

2. Work 2 double crochet

3. Chain 3

4. Work 3 double crochet into the same corner gap as in step 22

5. Chain 3 to the next gap

6. Work 3 double crochet

7. Chain 3 to next corner

8. Work 3 double crochet

9. Chain 3

10. Work 3 double crochet into that same corner gap from step 28

11. Repeat from step 25 once more

12. Chain 3

13. Slip stitch to close the round, pulling the yarn end firmly to make the knot tight

14. Cut your yarn, leaving a tail to weave in later

## ROUND 4:

1. Starting at any corner, chain 3

2. Work 2 double crochet

3. Chain 3

4. Work 3 double crochet into the same corner gap from step 35

5. Chain 3 to the next gap

6. Work 3 double crochet

7. Chain 3 to next gap

8. Work 3 double crochet

9. Chain 3 to next corner

10. Work 3 double crochet

11. Chain 3

12. Work 3 double crochet into that same corner gap from step 42

13. Chain 3 to the next gap

14. Work 3 double crochet

15. Chain 3 to the next gap

16. Work 3 double crochet

17. Chain 3 to the next corner

18. Repeat from step 44 once more

19. Slip stitch to close the round, pulling the yarn end firmly to make the knot tight

20. Cut your yarn, leaving a tail to weave in later.

## ROUND 5:

1. Starting at any corner, chain 3

2. Work 2 double crochet

3. Chain 3

4. Work 3 double crochet into the same corner gap as in step 55

5. Chain 3 to the next gap

6. Work 3 double crochet

7. Chain 3 to next gap

8. Work 3 double crochet

9. Chain 3 to next gap

10. Work 3 double crochet

11. Chain 3 to next corner

12. Work 3 double crochet

13. Chain 3

14. Work 3 double crochet into the same corner gap as in step 66

15. Chain 3 to the next gap

16. Work 3 double crochet

17. Chain 3 to next gap

18. Work 3 double crochet

19. Chain 3 to next gap

20. Work 3 double crochet

21. Repeat from step 65 once more

22. Slip stitch to close the round, pulling the yarn end firmly to make the knot tight.

23. Cut your yarn, leaving a tail to weave in later.

Once your granny bunting triangle is crocheted, pull the corners out to shape the triangle nicely and weave in all the yarn ends.

## THE LETTERS

Most letters are a mixture of pieces of 20 chain and 10 chain, though a couple have between 30 and 70 chain.

A: 2 x 20 chain, 1 x 10 chain

B: 3 x 20 chain

C: 1 x 40 chain

D: 1 x 30 chain, 1 x 20 chain

E: 1 x 20 chain, 3 x 10 chain

F: 1 x 20 chain, 2 x 10 chain

G: 1 x 30 chain, 1 x 10 chain

H: 2 x 20 chain, 1 x 10 chain

I: 1 x 20 chain

J: 1 x 30 chain

K: 1 x 20 chain, 2 x 10 chain

L: 1 x 20 chain, 1 x 10 chain

M: 2 x 20 chain, 2 x 10 chain

N: 3 x 20 chain

O: 1 x 50 chain

P: 2 x 20 chain

Q: 1 x 50 chain, 1 x 10 chain

R: 2 x 20 chain, 1 x 10 chain

S: 1 x 40 chain

T: 2 x 20 chain

U: 1 x 40 chain

V: 2 x 20 chain

W: 2 x 20 chain, 2 x 10 chain

X: 2 x 20 chain

Y: 1 x 20 chain, 2 x 10 chain

Z: 1 x 20 chain, 2 x 10 chain

&: 1 x 70 chain

!: 1 x 20 chain, 1 x 5 chain

#: 4 x 20 chain

1. Chain 10 (or 20, 30, 40, 50 or 70).

2. Double crochet into the 4th chain closest to your hook.

3. Double crochet into the 5th chain.

4. Repeat back down the line until you get to the end of the chain.

5. Cut your yarn and leave a long tail to weave in later.

6. Pin the letter pieces on the bunting.

7. Stitch around the edge of the letters to secure to bunting.

## TO MAKE UP

Lay the bunting out flat and secure each top corner to the next triangle with a few stitches.

Crochet 2 chains of 30, and stitch a chain to each outer corner to allow the bunting to tie up.

### Fat Activism

Fat activists are people of all sizes fighting against the pervasive idea that only thin, young, white people are beautiful and worthy. They resist the idea that being fat is a problem, instead, they feel that it's society's view of fat people that is problematic.

Fat activist Melissa McEwan writes, "The thing about 'love your body' campaigns for my fat self is that I can love my body all the f*** I want, but the bigger problem for me is other people hating my body."[1]

The slogan in this project was partly inspired by body image activist Amy Pence-Brown and her Boise Rad Fat Collective.

#bodydiversity #losehatenotweight #allbodiesaregoodbodies #fatactivism

---

1 McEwan, Melissa. "Fat and the Bikini Body Meme." *Shakesville*, June 3, 2014. http://www.shakesville.com/2014/06/fat-and-bikini-body-meme.html. (Accessed March 2018).

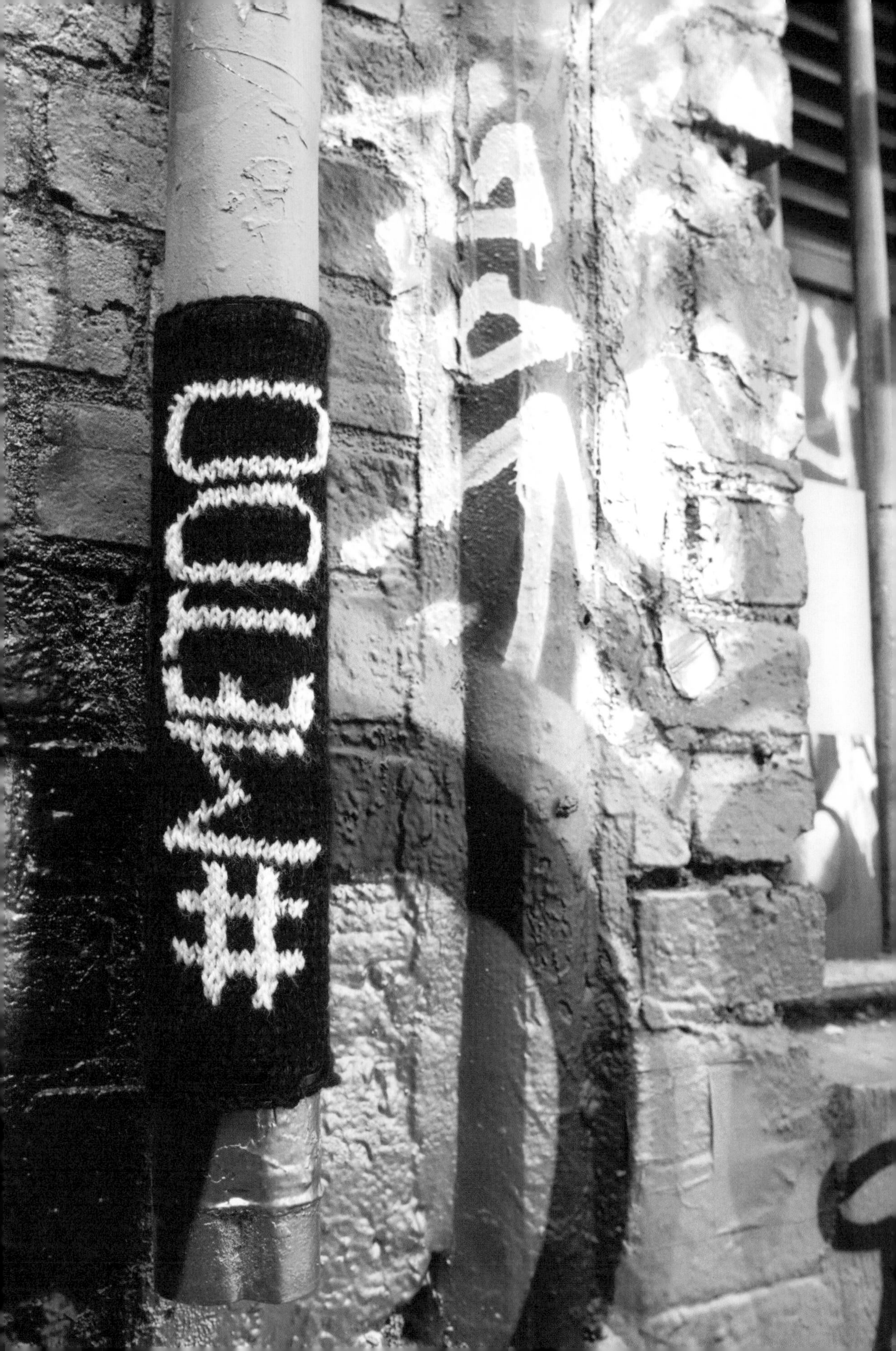
#MeToo

# Yarnbombs

**For a knitted yarn bomb**

*Knitting needles
(US 8 / metric 5mm / UK 6)[1]*

*Yarn—sports weight (8 ply)[2]*

*Darning or yarn needle*

*Zip/cable ties*

Public space is becoming more and more restricted by private corporations and government entities and is increasingly dominated by marketing companies. Public space should be our space, but it's often difficult to see it past all the billboards, security guards, and officials telling us to buy something or move on. Installing guerrilla works gives people a way to personalize the urban environment and reintroduce some humanity to our communal space. Yarnbombing is an excellent way to reclaim and beautify some of that space, or even to signify the fact that you were here, wending your way between the concrete alleys and towering steel and glass buildings. It is also just as effective in semi-rural and rural environments. If you can get there, you can yarnbomb it!

Yarn bombs can be knitted or crocheted. They can be as simple as a cozy around a tree or as complicated as a full set of clothes for a statue. They can have slogans stitched onto them once they're made or stitched into them as they're being created. Some are one color or multi-colored, others can be symbols or straight blocks. They can have pom-poms attached, tassels hanging off them, and soft sculptures or buttons and sequins stitched to them, or they can be as plain as you want. If you're looking for inspiration, check out the hashtags #yarnbombs or #yarnbombing to see the awesome creations people have made over the last few years.

This knitted yarnbomb uses the Fair Isle or Stranded technique of changing colors. If you don't know how to do this (or don't know how to knit), you can find instructions on page 179.

You can knit the #METOO yarnbomb or head further down to the second set of instructions to design your own.

1  For most knitting, I like thin needles and sports weight/8 ply yarn for a nice tight knit so the stuffing doesn't show through. However, for yarnbombs, I prefer thicker yarn and/or needles. This means it knits up quickly and can get out there fast. That works well unless you want a lot of stitches to accommodate a complicated design or a lot of words, in which case a thinner yarn and thinner needles will help you accomplish this.

2  It's hard to estimate how much yarn you'll need because it depends on how wide you want to make your yarn bomb. However, a single ball of yarn should be more than enough for the main color of this project and certainly enough for the secondary color.

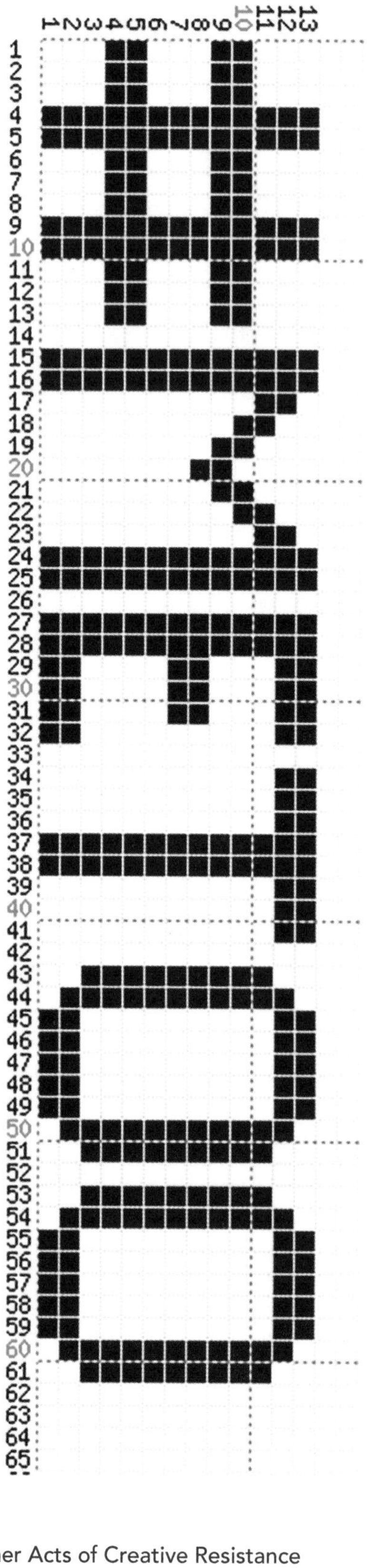

## DIRECTIONS

1. The easiest place to start is with a pole. Measure the diameter of the pole and decide what height you want your yarnbomb to be. If this is your first few times knitting, smaller is probably better. The pole I have my eye on is a street sign which measures 8 inches (20 centimeters) around.

2. Next, knit a little swatch to know how tight or loose your knit will be. Cast on 10 stitches and knit a couple of rows. Once it's done, measure how wide it is. My swatch of 10 stitches is 2 inches (5 centimeters) across. I need the yarnbomb to be 8 inches (20 centimeters) across. The pole of 8 inches (20 centimeters) divided by my swatch of 2 inches (5 centimeters) equals 4. Basically, I need my knitting to be 4 times wider than my swatch. This means my yarn bomb needs to be 40 stitches across. This may be different for you.

3. The #METOO pattern provided is 13 stitches across. I needed to add 27 stitches (12 and 13 respectively to each side of the design) to make it up to 40 stitches. You might need to add more or less. You also might like to add some stitches top and bottom to give the design more space. For this yarn bomb, I added 10 rows at each end.

4. Contrast-color stitches are shown in red. Border stitches are shown outside of asterisks. To adjust the size of the border to suit your area, increase or decrease the number of stitches outside of asterisks.

## CAST ON YOUR NUMBER OF STITCHES

| | |
|---|---|
| Row 1: | K2*, k3, k2, k3, k2, k3, *k2 |
| Row 2: | K2*, p3, p2, p3, p2, p3, *k2 |
| Row 3: | K2*, k3, k2, k3, k2, k3, *k2 |
| Row 4: | K2*, p13, *k2 |
| Row 5: | K2*, k13, *k2 |
| Row 6: | K2*, p3, p2, p3, p2, p3, *k2 |
| Row 7: | As for row 1. |
| Row 8: | As for row 2. |
| Row 9: | As for row 5. |
| Row 10: | As for row 4. |
| Row 11: | As for row 1. |
| Row 12: | As for row 2. |
| Row 13: | As for row 1. |
| Row 14: | K2*, p13, *k2 |

| Row 15: | As for row 5. |
| Row 16: | As for row 4. |
| Row 17: | K2*, k11, k2, *k2 |
| Row 18: | K2*, p2, p2, p9, *k2 |
| Row 19: | K2*, k8, k2, k3, *k2 |
| Row 20: | K2*, p4, p2, p7, *k2 |
| Row 21: | As for row 19. |
| Row 22: | As for row 18. |
| Row 23: | K2*, k10, k2, k1, *k2. |
| Row 24: | As for row 4. |
| Row 25: | As for row 5. |
| Row 26: | As for row 14. |
| Row 27: | As for row 5. |
| Row 28: | As for row 4. |
| Row 29: | K2*, k2, k4, k2, k3, k2, *k2 |
| Row 30: | K2*, p2, p3, p2, p4, p2, *k2 |
| Row 31: | As for row 29. |
| Row 32: | K2*, p2, p9, p2, *k2 |
| Row 33: | K2*, k13, *k2 |
| Row 34: | K2*, p2, p9, *k2 |
| Row 35: | K2*, k11, k2, *k2 |
| Row 36: | As for row 34. |
| Row 37: | As for row 5. |
| Row 38: | As for row 4. |
| Row 39: | As for row 35. |
| Row 40: | As for row 34. |
| Row 41: | As for row 35. |
| Row 42: | As for row 14. |
| Row 43: | K2*, k2, k9, k2, *k2 |
| Row 44: | K2*, p1, p11, p1, *k2 |
| Row 45: | K2*, k2, k9, k2, *k2 |
| Row 46: | K2*, k2, p2, p9, p2, *k2 |

| Row 47: | As for row 45. |
| Row 48: | As for row 46. |
| Row 49: | As for row 45. |
| Row 50: | As for row 44. |
| Row 51: | As for row 43. |
| Row 52: | As for row 14. |
| Row 53–61: | As for row 43–52. |

## DIRECTIONS

### DESIGNING YOUR OWN KNITTED YARNBOMB

1. To make your own yarnbomb, follow steps 1 and 2 above to figure out the size your knitting will need to be.

2. Now you need to grid it out. There's a blank grid on page 214 you can photocopy. If you need more squares, photocopy a couple and tape them together. Alternatively, you can do a quick internet search for "customizable printable grid," there are heaps out there. Select the number of stitches across for the horizontal row and the number of rows high for your vertical row and print it out.

3. Now you're all ready to design your yarn bomb. Sketch it out using a pencil so you can erase any mistakes.

4. Once you're happy with it, you can either use your grid to knit it up or you can write out the instructions based on your grid, if you prefer working from instructions rather than a graphic.

### TO INSTALL ON A POLE

1. Slide a zip/cable tie through the row of stitches at the top and bottom.

2. Wrap your design around the pole.

3. Zip up the zip tie.

4. Cut any excess length of the zip/cable tie off with scissors or pliers.

5. Run a couple of stitches down the sides of the cross stitch to secure it more firmly.

## #metoo

The Me Too project was founded by activist and community organizer Tarana Burke in 2006 as part of a grassroots campaign to help unify those who have experienced sexual assault, especially in underprivileged communities. In an interview with *Ebony*, Burke stated she never envisioned it as a hashtag, instead it was created as a "… catchphrase to be used from survivor to survivor to let folks know they were not alone and that a movement for radical healing was happening and possible."[1] On the 15th of October, 2017, the phrase went viral when actor Alyssa Milano encouraged people who had been sexually harassed or assaulted to reply to her tweet with the phrase "me too." It spread across social media and was used over 100,000 times within twenty-four hours. Although the hashtag campaign has been criticized by some for putting the onus on the survivor or putting pressure on survivors to tell their stories, others find publicly using the phrase empowering.

#metoo metoo.support

1 Hill, Zara. "A Black Woman Created the 'Me Too' Campaign Against Sexual Assault 10 Years Ago." *Ebony*, October 18, 2017. www.ebony.com/news-views/black-woman-me-too-tarana-burke-alyssa-milano. (Accessed March 2018.)

# CHAPTER THREE

# Cross Stitch and Embroidery

There's a lot of odd ideas about embroidery and cross stitch that I want to debunk here before we get started. While some crafters maintain attention to detail and finished works, our aim as craftivists is to clearly communicate our message. Perfectly finished works take time, delay your intervention, and demand you conform to an aesthetic standard inherited from patriarchal social constructs of excellence. Getting it out there is more important than getting it perfect.

*"The back has to look as neat as the front."* Totally untrue! It doesn't matter if your thread gets tangled at the back or if you travel the thread all the way across the back to make a stitch and then travel it all the way back again. Do what you need to do to stitch the letters on.

*"With cross stitch, you have to always stitch the same way (diagonally)."* Nope. If your first "X'" has the left to right stroke done first and the right to left done second, and the second "X" is the other way around, don't worry about it! It's the message that's important, not the neatness of the stitches.

*"All the stitches have to be perfect."* Wrong again! If some of your stitches are a little wobbly or if some are fatter or thinner than others, that's okay! Like everything else in this book, this is a handmade item, and there's bound to be some differences between the stitching. It just makes it unique.

And finally, if you're embarking on designing your own stitching project, there are websites out there where you can load up images and photos to convert to cross stitch charts, so if you have a logo or a symbol, or a more complicated pattern or photo you can't figure out on your own, head to the internet!

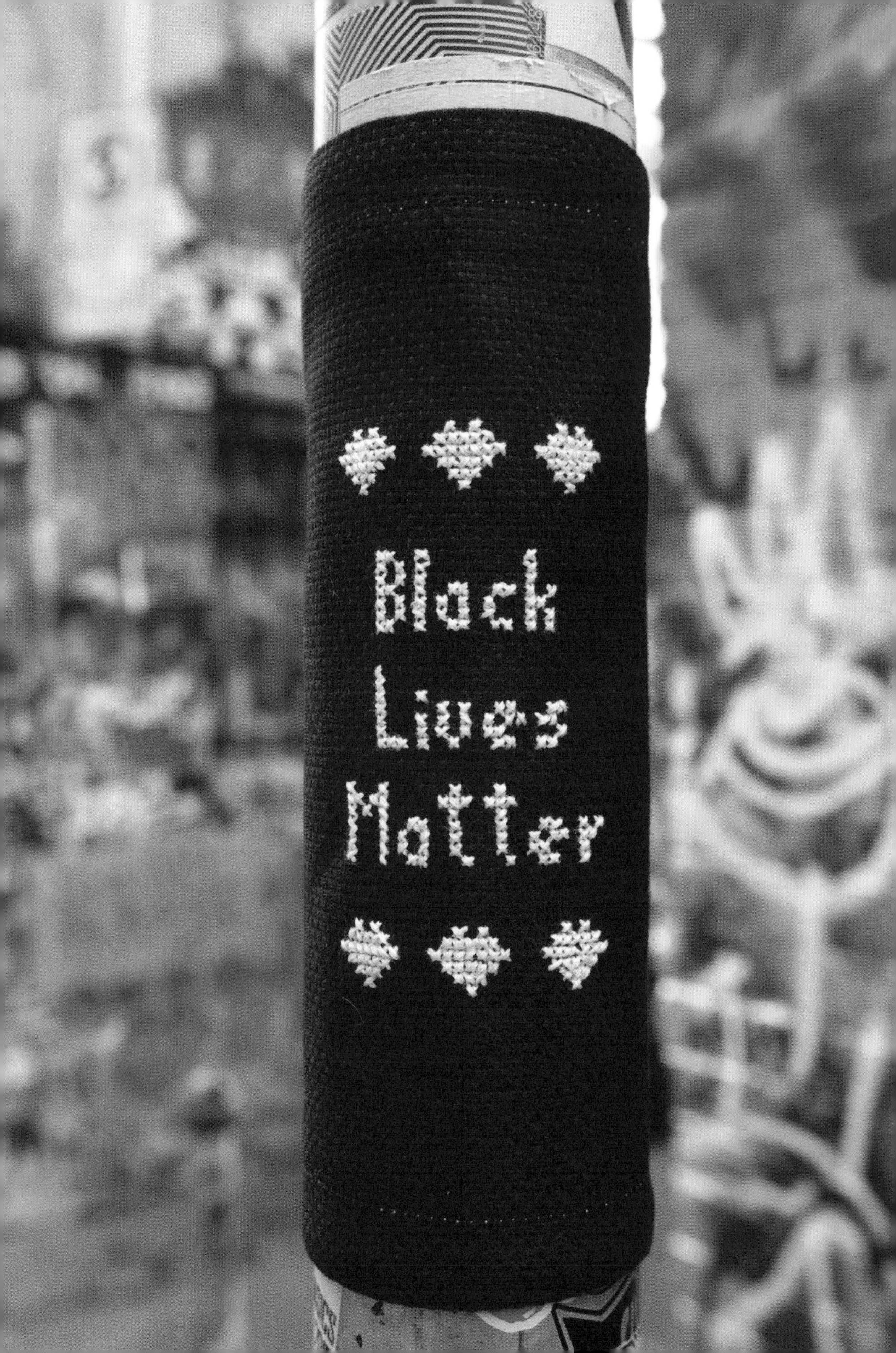
Black
Lives
Matter

# Cross Stitch

## WHAT YOU'LL NEED

*Embroidery hoop*

*Needle*

*Scissors*

*Embroidery thread
(a single skein is enough for
a number of cross stitches)*

*Aida cloth
(I've used a piece 8 inches
(20 centimeters) x 10 inches
(25 centimeters) to ensure it
wraps around the pole.
If you're not sure,
measure your pole first to
get the size right.)*

*Zip/cable ties*

These cross stitch works were originally designed as public protest pieces to be put out on poles, trees, fences, park benches, or anywhere else outside where you can attach one. But they can also be framed and installed as an inside protest as well!

If you are stitching the example "Black Lives Matter" pattern, read on, but if you want to design your own, head down to the second set of instructions. If you haven't cross stitched before, you can head over to the cross stitch instructions on page 189.

The Black Lives Matter cross stitch has 278 stitches in it and ends up being around 2½ inches (6 centimeters) by 4 inches (10 centimeters) depending on what size aida cloth you use.

In cross stitches that have a lot of space to fill, some people like to do a single diagonal stitch all across the row in one direction and then come back filling in the second diagonal stitch. But for this style of cross stitch, where only a few stitches are done and the background is left blank, I find it's better to complete each cross as you go.

## DIRECTIONS

1. Cut a length of embroidery thread about the length of your forearm; any longer, and it can get tangled quickly.

2. Embroidery thread is made of 6 strands, so divide it in half, 3 strands each. This makes the stitching easier and makes your thread go further.

3. Fold your aida cloth in half lengthways and finger press along the folded seam. Then fold it widthwise and finger press that seam to give you the middle of the cloth. If you've designed your own pattern, count in from the side and down from the top to find the middle of your pattern. In the Black Lives Matter pattern, I've placed a green square right in the middle of the pattern for you.

4. Now it's time to cross stitch. Following a cross stitch pattern is just like finding a point on a map. If you're not confident, feel free to mark the pattern out first with a washable fabric marker, fading fabric marker or even a light pencil on the back of the cloth.

5. Once your design is done, you'll need a little sleeve at the top and the bottom of the design to slide the zip/cable tie through. Turn the cross stitch wrong side up and then fold the sleeve 1 inch (2½ centimeters) over and stitch down.

6. If your fabric is a little wrinkled, or is holding the finger press fold or embroidery hoop impression, you can iron it. To do this, place a towel onto your ironing board and place the cross stitch on it wrong side up. Iron carefully around the stitches. If you need to iron the fabric where the stitches are, place another towel over the stitches and press the iron down. Pick up the iron, move it to the next part and press it down again. Don't slide the iron around like you would normally, this can pull the stitches and twist your design. If your cloth still has creases, you can also dampen the cloth a little and iron again.

## TO INSTALL

1. Slide a zip/cable tie through the top and bottom sleeve

2. Wrap your design around the pole.

3. Zip the zip/cable tie closed tightly against the pole.

4. Cut any excess length of the zip/cable tie off with scissors or pliers.

5. (Optional) You can also run a couple of stitches down the open sides of the cross stitch at the back of the pole to secure it more firmly. Yarnbombs are also secured this way, check out the photo on page 60.

## DESIGN YOUR OWN CROSS STITCH

If you're keen to design your own, on page 216, there is the whole cross stitch alphabet and some extra symbols for you to use, and on page 214, there is a blank grid.

When planning out a cross stitch pattern, there are a couple of things to remember. You need to know how many stitches wide each letter is, and you also need to plan for a space between each letter to ensure they don't run into each other and make the design unreadable. Make sure you count from the edge of the letter—for example, the cross bar of a "t" hangs out further than its downward stroke.

1. First, decide on your slogan. If this is your first cross stitch, something shorter is better.

2. Write it out on a piece of scrap paper.

3. Now you need to plan your pattern. Refer to the alphabet and count how many stitches wide each of your letters will be. For example, capital "B" is 3 stitches wide, and a lower case "w" is 5 stitches wide. Make a note of each width under your slogan.

4. Remember, there will also need to be a single space between each so they don't run into each other. You'll also need 3 spaces between each word to make them clear. If your slogan spans several lines, you'll need 3 spaces between each line.

### Black Lives Matter

#BlackLivesMatter was started in 2014 by three African American women—Alicia Garza, Patrisse Cullors, and Opal Tometi—after a white Neighbourhood Watch volunteer was acquitted of charges in the death of unarmed black teenager Trayvon Martin. Since then, the movement has grown into a global network which leads campaigns, protests, and calls for legislative reform. On their website, they write: *"We are working for a world where Black people are no longer systematically targeted by governments for demise. We affirm our humanity, our contributions to this society, and our resilience in the face of deadly oppression."*

blacklivesmatter.com  #blacklivesmatter

## Always Was, Always Will Be

"Always was, always will be" is a shortened version of the phrase "Always was, always will be Aboriginal land," which refers to the facts that Indigenous Australians never ceded sovereignty of their country to the colonizing English and that no Australian government has ever entered into a treaty with Indigenous Australians to live and work on their land. This cross stitch also features the Australian Aboriginal flag, which was designed in 1971 by indigenous artist Harold Thomas, who is descended from the Luritja people of Central Australia. The black stripe represents the Aboriginal people of Australia, the yellow circle is the Sun, the giver of life and protector, and the red stripes represent the red earth, the red ochre used in ceremonies, and the Aboriginal people's spiritual relation to the land.

#alwayswasalwayswillbe

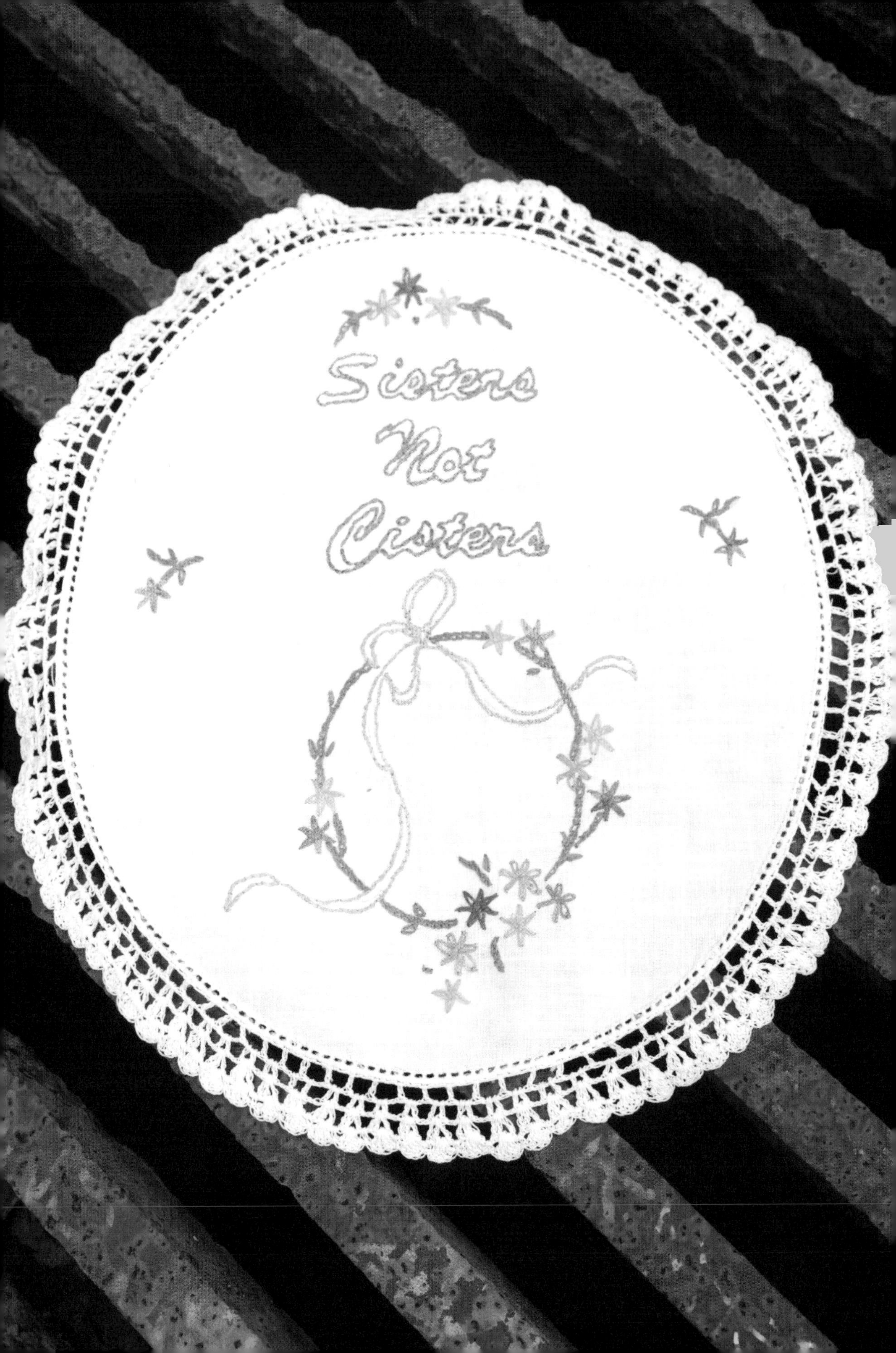
Sisters
Not
Cisters

# Embroidery on Reclaimed Doilies

## WHAT YOU'LL NEED

*Doily*

*Pen*

*Embroidery thread
(a single skein will do a
number of doilies)*

*Needle*

*Scissors*

**Not needed but handy**

*An embroidery hoop*

There's already so much fabric in the world, why buy more when you can use what's already out there? Any fabric you can find can be used for this, although fragile or see-through fabric will pose more of a challenge.

This project is a quick little one using doilies from charity shops (or purchased online).

The slogan is entirely up to you and can incorporate anything that is already stitched to the doily.

Instead of telling you how to make your project, since there's so many variables in this one, I'll tell you how I did mine.

For the main item, I wanted to stitch "Sisters Not Cisters" and so looked online for a doily with pink and blue flowers to represent the pink, blue, and white colors of the Trans Pride flag.

I was feeling brave, so I was going to sketch the writing straight onto the doily, but then I decided that I wanted a fancier font than I could draw freehand. I chose a font I wanted (Brush Script MT), made sure it was the right size by holding the doily up to the screen (90 pt), and printed it out. To transfer it to the doily, I taped the printout to my window on a sunny day and placed the doily on top to trace the image. You can trace it with a soft pencil, a light colored thin line pen, or a special fabric pen that fades after 24 hours or will wash out once you're done. You might think you want to skip the printing out step and trace the image straight from your computer screen, but screens are very delicate and pressing hard on them can damage them, so it's safer to print it out and stick it to a window.

Once my fancy font was drawn onto my doily, I stitched the words with a simple backstitch. If you don't know how to backstitch, there are instructions on page 191, but also feel free to get as fancy as you like! You can search online for embroidery stitches. There are hundreds to choose from.

The smaller doily of the witch was a little more work. I was interested in portraying the medieval mythology of the witch, and specifically the idea that they used Deadly Nightshade for flying potions. This project was intended as barter in exchange for a friend looking after our dog one weekend. You can read more about barters on page 168.

I searched for a doily with pointy petalled flowers and found this one in a bargain box in an antique store. I unpicked the flowers and seed pods, which were white and green respectively, and restitched them in dark purple and black to suggest Deadly Nightshade.

For the witch, I searched online for medieval woodcuts of witches until I found one I liked, and then resized and printed out the image as I did with the "Sisters" doily listed above. Then I stitched around the image. I chose purple and black for the witch to mirror the colors of the Nightshade below her.

Done!

## SOME OTHER THINGS TO THINK ABOUT

Your slogan doesn't have to match up with whatever is embroidered on the doily. You can unpick parts or add an embroidered image to the doily too (such as the witch above); however, sometimes you find doilies with pre-embroidered images that are just perfect for your slogan.

For example, a doily with cake/sandwiches could be for such slogans as "Riots Not Diets"; "F your Beauty Standards"; or "Eat all the cake you want, take all the space you need."

A doily with a couple of riding bikes could have "bikes not bombs" stitched on it.

A doily with a tea cup on it could be for "equaliTEA."

A doily with lavender or purple flowers could be used for "Lavender Menace."

And if you need to iron your embroidery once it's done, head over to the previous cross stitch project on page 69; step six can be used for embroidery as well as cross stitch.

## Sisters Not Cisters

The term "transgender" refers to people who identify with gender/s other than the one they were assigned at birth. The opposite of this is "cisgender," meaning a person who does identify with their assigned gender. However, there are some people who think that transwomen are not real women, and transmen aren't real men. This slogan pushes back against that idea and proclaims that transwomen are just as real women as cisgender women.

#trans, #transgender

## Witches

In second wave feminism women started reclaiming the word "witch." Often used as a slur against women, the feminists looked to the origin of the word, the healer or wise woman, and reclaimed it. Religious scholar Cynthia Eller writes, "By choosing this symbol, feminists were identifying themselves with everything women were taught not to be: ugly, aggressive, independent, and malicious. Feminists took this symbol and molded it—not into the fairy tale "good witch," but into a symbol of female power, knowledge, independence, and martyrdom."[1]

1 Edwards, Trista. "W.I.T.C.H: THE 1960s Women's LIBERATION GROUP & WHY WE NEED a NEW WITCH." *Luna Luna*, January 18, 2017. www.lunalunamagazine.com/blog/witch-womens-lib. (Accessed March 2018.)

# CHAPTER FOUR

# Sewing

The next few projects are all sewing projects. Each can be done by hand or by machine, according to your own preference. The banners and pennants use felt for their design. One of the things I like most about felt is that it doesn't fray, so it doesn't need hemming. It's also cheap and can be found in most fabric and craft stores (and often in charity stores too). But feel free to use any fabric you wish. If you're using fabric that frays, you can hem it or use the appliqué method from the Quilted Patch project on page 106.

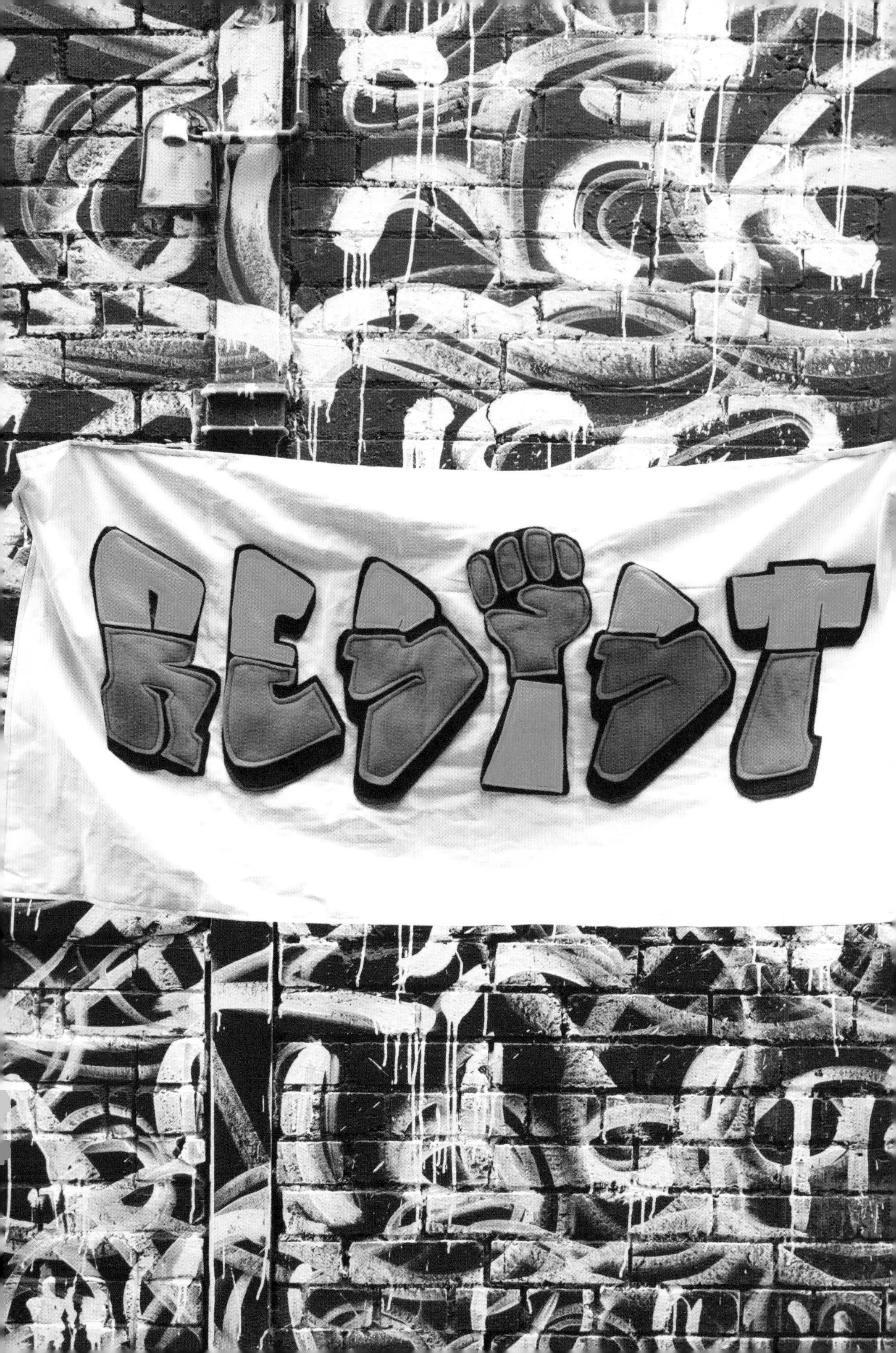
RESIST

# Protest Banners

*Pattern (pages 217-221)*

*Felt (for RESIST, you'll need 6 black sheets of felt, 4 purple and 3 pink)*

*Background fabric (for RESIST, you'll need around 42 inches (107 centimeters) by 21 inches (53½ centimeters))*

*Scissors*

*Pins*

*Sewing machine/sewing needle/fabric glue/hot glue (whichever you're using)*

This project is a simple one which makes a bold statement. The pattern for RESIST is on pages 217-221, but of course you can choose any slogan you like for your banner. You can also add symbols and images if you wish. If you're using more letters than the six letters in RESIST or adding symbols, make them a smaller size, as you don't want your banner to be giant! (Unless you do, in which case, you'll need to find some buddies to help you carry it.) If you're using felt, it can be glued on, sewn using a machine, or hand sewn.

Felt comes in rolls or in sheets about the size of a sheet of paper. I like to buy the paper-sized (8½" x 11") ones to make things easier. If your slogan is short, enlarge each letter to a single page size—that way, each letter will fit on a felt sheet.

## DIRECTIONS

1. Photocopy the pattern and cut out each shape, or print and cut out your letters. If they have a shadow like the RESIST letters in this example, cut out the whole letter including the shadow.

2. Pin the letter to a felt sheet and cut out. If you're doing RESIST, pin the letter to a black sheet of felt and cut out the whole letter. Remember to cut two S's!

3. Once you've cut out all the letters in black, return to your paper letter and cut out the top and bottom parts of the pattern.

4. Pin the top of each letter to the pink felt (or whichever color you choose) and cut them out.

5. Pin the bottom of each letter to the purple felt (or again, whichever color you've chosen) and cut those out.

6. Pin the top and bottom part of each letter to the black shadow and stitch down (I don't mind a little bit of the black peeking out between the middle). You can use a sewing machine, hand stitching, or glue, whichever is your preference.

7. Pin each completed letter to the background fabric. You can either overlap them or space them out so they don't touch each other, it's up to you how you want your banner to look!

8. Affix the letters to the fabric, again with a sewing machine, hand sewing or glue, however you like.

9. If using slower drying glue, leave somewhere overnight to dry. If using hot glue, be careful! That stuff can burn your fingers very easily! But it will harden and cool pretty quickly.

10. If you want the banner to last for a number of protests, then hem the edges of the banner so it doesn't fray (unless fraying is part of your banner aesthetic).

## TO FINISH OFF

There are a couple of ways to finish your banner off. You can use it as is, or you can add a couple of things to make it easier to hold.

1. You can sew a ribbon or a thinly hemmed piece of fabric straight across each top corner at the back to give you some handles for it.

2. If you sew a sleeve down each side, you can slide a piece of wood or broom stick into them to act as poles. Measure the diameter of your intended pole. The measurement for the sleeve will be twice that diameter. Fold each side edge over to your measurement, pin, and sew. Sew the top closed so the banner doesn't just slide down the stick.

3. If your banner is huge, it's also good to cut out semi-circular flaps about the size of a coffee mug to let the wind though. This way it doesn't turn into a sail and drag you down the street.

Of course, pennants and banners can be painted too. Draw the symbol straight onto the banner (use a light pencil for light fabrics and chalk or a white pencil for darker fabrics) and paint it in. The best paint to use for this is acrylic, which is cheap, readily available, and waterproof once dry. Fabric paint works just as well if you happen to have any. Just remember to protect the table under your fabric with plastic—a cut open plastic bag works perfectly.

## Anarchist Symbol

Anarchy is a political ideology that advocates for a society without rules or non-hierarchical societies. There are a lot of different styles of anarchy, however, common across them all is the idea that government is unnecessary and even harmful to society. The idea of anarchy has been around since the sixth century BCE and can be found in the works of the Taoist philosopher Lao-tzu. This anarchy symbol consists of a letter "A" surrounded by the letter "O." The A stands for Anarchy and the O stands for Order. Together they stand for "society seeks order in anarchy," a phrase written by Pierre-Joseph Proudhon in his 1840 book *What Is Property?*

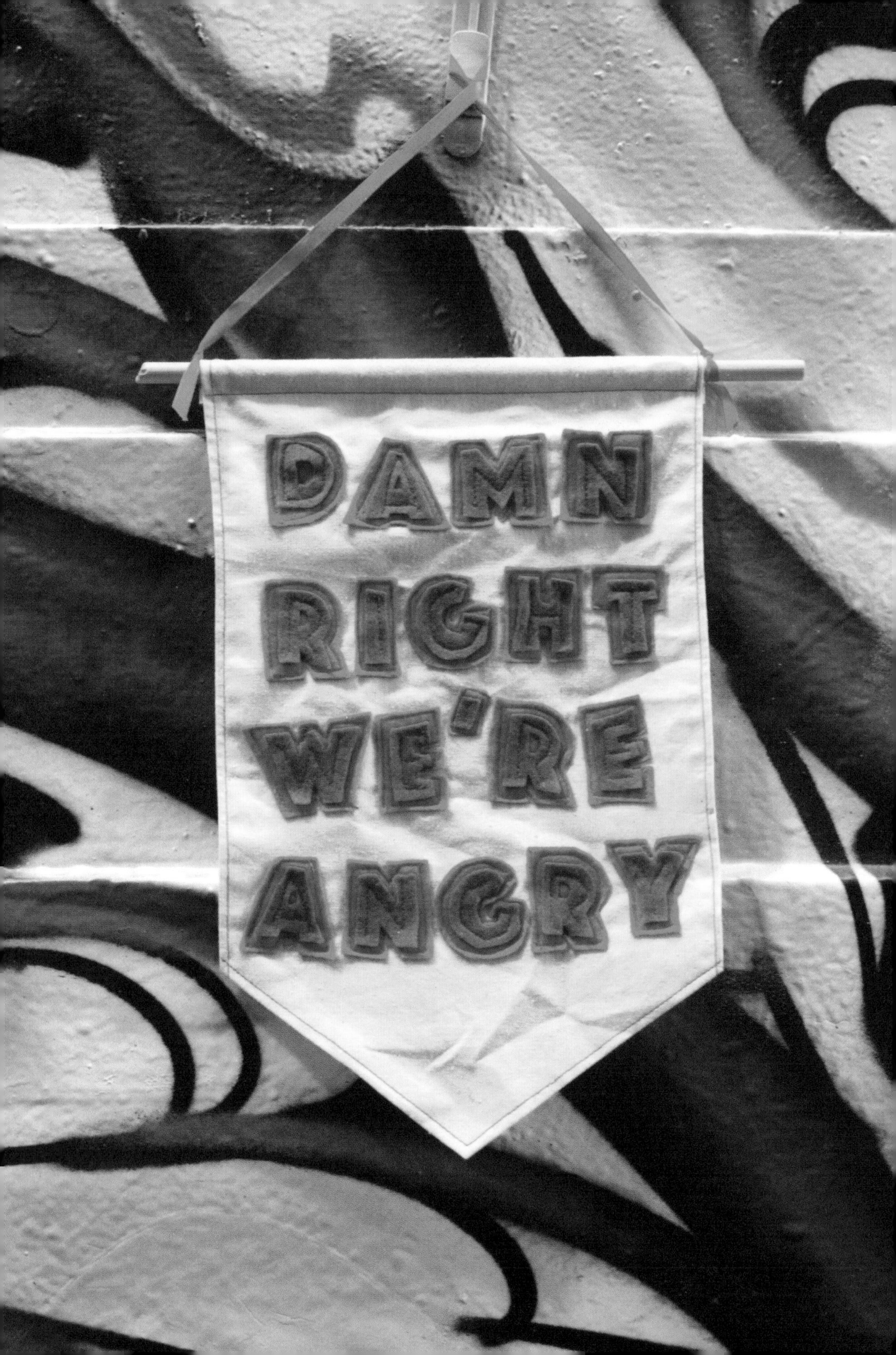
DAMN
RIGHT
WE'RE
ANGRY

# Pennant

## WHAT YOU'LL NEED

*Pattern (pages 222-223)*

*Non-stretch fabric,
16 inches (40 centimeters)
by 8 inches (21 centimeters)*

*Small dowel rod
(or chopstick, knitting
needle, or found stick.
If you're making a thinner
pennant, even a spare
pencil will work)*

*Scissors*

*Pins*

*Felt*

*Ribbon approximately
24 inches
(61 centimeters) long*

*Sewing machine*

*Marker or pencil*

These pennants are super easy to make and come in two styles—a hanging pennant banner and a flag style pennant that you can wave when you take your cause to the streets.

This pennant's pattern is on page 222, or you can design your own. You can use any font you like, but it's better to use a less fancy font for your first one—fonts with swirls and curlicues are harder to cut out in felt. You can also abandon the computer entirely and hand draw your lettering. Go old school if that suits you better! The dimensions of the pennant banner given below are for a single 8½" by 11" (or A4) page.

Make sure to iron your fabric first before you start—it's much harder to iron it once everything is sewn onto it. If your iron has a steam feature or occasionally leaks water, you should be aware that the color of felt can sometimes run (eeek!).

## DIRECTIONS

1. Photocopy pattern and cut out main shape, then pin to fabric and cut out.

2. (If you're designing your own, fold your fabric in half lengthways and measure 12 inches (30 centimeters) from the top along the edge. Draw a line from this point to the point where the fabric is folded in the middle at the bottom, and then cut along this line to get the pointed bottom edge of the pennant.)

3. To seam the pennant, fold each edge over ¼ inch (½ centimeter) and pin. Then sew.

4. Now for the sleeve at the top where the dowel rod sits. Measure the diameter of your dowel. Thinner is better for this project. My dowel was 1/3 inch (1 centimeter), so the measurement we're using for the sleeve is twice that, or 2/3 inch (2 centimeters). Fold the top edge over to your measurement, pin, and sew.

5. Cut out your paper letters, pin them to the felt, and cut out.

6. If you're using printed fabric for the background of the pennant, a single color for your letters is fine, but plain fabric pennants can look great with a second, thicker layer of a different color. I'm loving the red and purple together of the main pennant!

7. Position your letters on your pennant and pin.

8. Stitch around your letters. Choose a contrasting color thread if you're keen for it. If doing the double layer, pin the top layer letter to the bottom layer letter and run a single line of stitching through the middle of the letter. Then pin it to the pennant and stitch around the edge of the bottom letter.

9. Insert the dowel into the sleeve and tie the ribbon to each end.

10. Done! Hang it somewhere awesome.

To make the flag pennant is a very similar process, except the flag measures 8 inches (20 centimeters) long and 15 inches (38 centimeters) wide. The pattern for this one is on page 223, but feel free to design your own, which can face left, right, or down.

Unlike the other pennant, I hand sewed this flag pennant. This was for two reasons. One was because the letters got quite small near the point; I figured it would be tricky to use my machine, and I wanted all the stitching to look the same. The second was because it was sewn on a relaxing evening and my television is in a different room than my sewing machine.

To hang it, I've simply sewn small loops at the top corner and one more at the pointy end. If your flag points downward, sew these loops at the top instead.

## Not Your Inspiration

Stella Young (1982–2014) was an Australian journalist, comedian, outspoken disability activist, and wheelchair user. On her twitter bio she wrote, "Writer. Comedian. Knitter. Crip. Inspiration boner killer." One of the focuses of her activism was the idea that disabled people are viewed as "inspiring" just for doing regular things like getting out of bed in the morning, going shopping, or making artwork. Young was having none of it. She even coined a phrase for those photos that do the rounds on social media of disabled people doing regular things captioned with inspiring quotes—"Inspiration porn." In an article in 2012, she wrote, "… using these images as feel-good tools, as 'inspiration,' is based on an assumption that the people in them have terrible lives, and that it takes some extra kind of pluck or courage to live them. …"[1] In a radio interview she elaborated further: "It speaks to this kind of assumption that people with disabilities are 'brave' because our lives are horrible, and that's not true at all."[2]

Stella did a TEDxSydney talk about this bluntly titled, "I'm not your inspiration, thank you very much." You can see a video of Stella's TED talk at:

https://www.ted.com/talks/stella_young_i_m_not_your_inspiration_thank_you_very_much/

(The link includes a transcript.)

The new wheelchair symbol was created by Sara Hendren and Brian Glenny as a guerrilla street art activist project in 2011. Since then it has been adopted by a number of states and institutions around the world.

1 Young, Stella. "We're not here for your inspiration." ABC's *Ramp Up*, July 2, 2012. http://www.abc.net.au/rampup/articles/2012/07/02/3537035.htm. (Accessed March 2018.)

2 Bannister, Brooke. "Who are you? Stella Young." ABC's *Radio Perth*, February 29, 2012. http://www.abc.net.au/local/audio/2012/02/29/3442495.htm. (Accessed March 2018.)

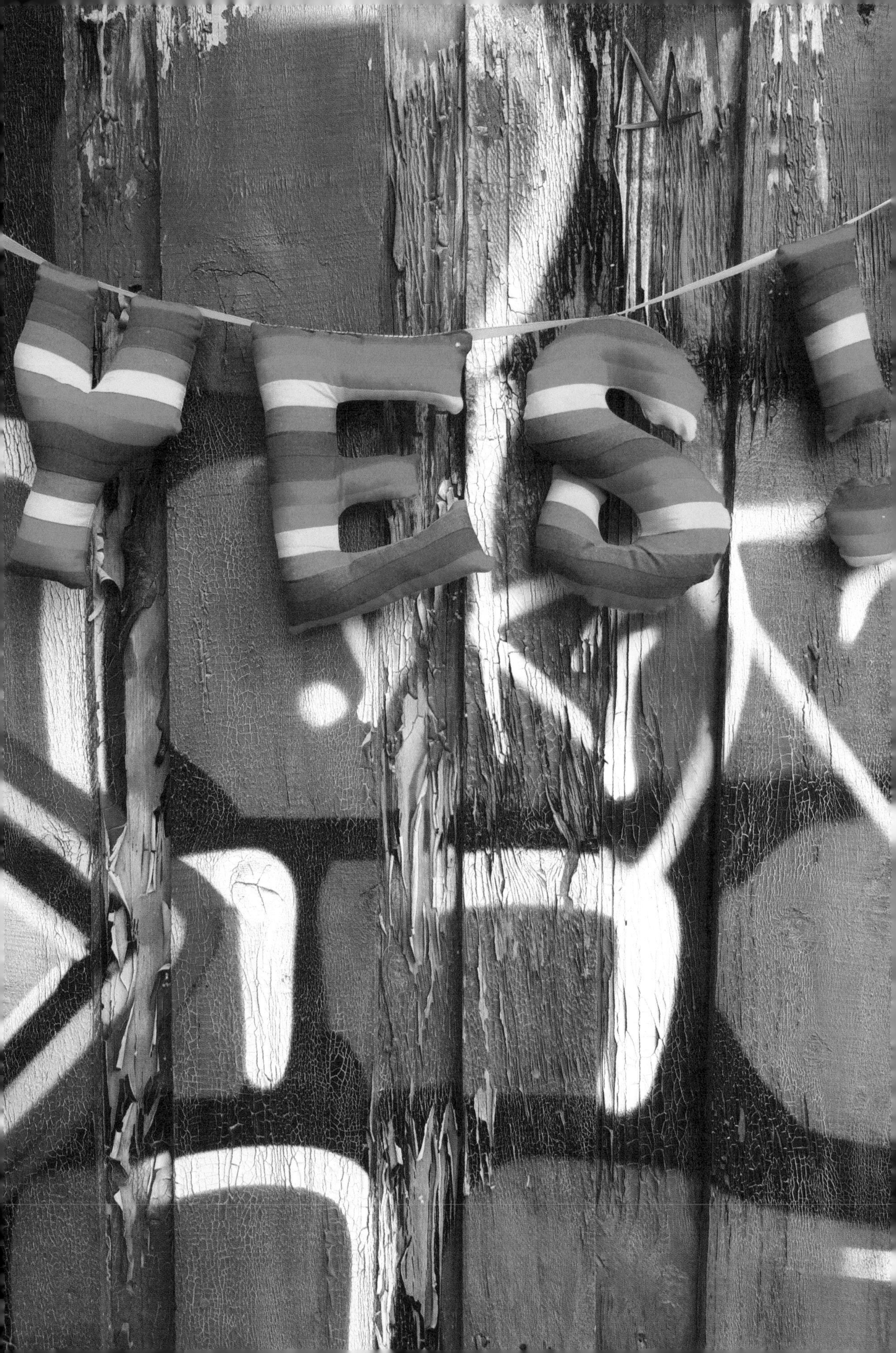
YES

# Soft Sculpture Bunting

## WHAT YOU'LL NEED

*Paper for the pattern*

*Permanent marker or pen*

*Scissors*

*Fabric*

*Stuffing*

*Ribbon—the length of all your letters spaced out plus around 24 inches (60 centimeters)*

*Needle and thread*

*Pins*

I found this idea in a 1970s Christmas craft book from a charity store. This just proves that any craft can be used for activism and that it's always worth flicking through old craft books in charity shops for interesting ideas.

This YES was so simple I haven't provided the pattern; I hand drew the letters, and you can too. You can also print them out using a computer if you're not into the hand drawn style. For ease of construction and legibility, I suggest choosing a simple font without any fancy swirls, flicks, or serifs. Try to find a wider font for this project, or use the "bold" option to make it thicker and make the letters stand out more.

## DIRECTIONS

This is much easier to do on a sewing machine than to stitch by hand, but do what works for you!

1. Decide on your word or phrase and draw or print out the letters. I find fitting two letters to a single page is a good guideline, but it depends on how big you want the letters and how long your words are. It's best to stick to either all capitals or all lower case as the mix of heights when using both can look a little odd in the finished product.

2. Place your fabric right sides together. Pin the paper letters to the fabric, making sure to leave a little gap between them.

3. Cut out your letters, making sure to include a seam allowance. I like to leave ¼ inch (½ centimeter) for seams.

4. Sew around the letter, leaving part of the piece unsewn so you can turn it right side out. In letters with a hole in them, such as O, P, D, B, or Q, etc., you can sew around the entire outer edge and then use the inside hole to turn them through. For other letters, leave around a 2-inch (5-centimeter) gap near the top.

5.  Before you turn the letter right side out, you need to clip any excess fabric away from any corners or curves—but be careful to not cut your stitching! For clipping guidelines, check out the instructions on page 178.

6.  Turn your letters right side out. You may need the top of a knitting needle or the end of a pen to push the corners out properly.

7.  Stuff your letters. You should stuff them firmly enough that they don't sag, but not so firmly that they are very heavy.

8.  Tuck the seam allowance into the open gap, then pin and stitch closed.

9.  Lay your letters on a flat surface and pin the ribbon across the top of each, making sure there is an even amount of ribbon at both ends to hang the finished piece.

10.  Pick up the ribbon and check that all your letters are hanging correctly and that there's an even space between each.

11.  Once you're satisfied with the placement, stitch each letter to the ribbon. For letters with two or more top edges, such as W, M, or Y, it's best to sew both edges to the ribbon so the letter doesn't hang at an odd angle (unless of course you're all about odd angles).

12.  If you include punctuation such as an exclamation point or question mark, the dot of the mark is held in place with a couple of long stitches on either side between the dot and the letter.

13.  If required, the ends of the ribbon can be sewn together in a loop for ease of hanging.

If you like the messier look, or you want to make these faster, sew them together on the outside rather than the inside. You'll get a raw rough edge around the words which will give them quite a different look. An additional advantage to sewing them this way is that you don't need to hand sew them closed once you've stuffed them, you can use your machine.

1. Follow step one above.

2. Place your fabric wrong sides together. Pin the letters to the fabric, making sure to leave a little gap between them.

3. Cut out your letters, making sure to include the ¼-inch (2-centimeter) seam allowance.

4. Sew around the letter, leaving part of the piece unsewn so you can stuff them— around a 2-inch (5-centimeter) gap near the top.

5. Stuff your letters. You should stuff them firmly enough that they don't sag, but not so firmly that they are very heavy.

6. Sew the hole closed using your sewing machine or by hand.

7. Follow steps 10–14 above to finish your bunting off.

## YES

At the time I was writing this book, the Australian government was conducting the "Australian Marriage Law Postal Survey" asking the citizens of Australia if they thought same-sex marriage should be legalized in Australia. This postal survey was non-binding (meaning the government doesn't have to act on it), non-compulsory (voting in Australia is required, but this survey was not), voluntary (meaning you didn't have to participate if you didn't want to). The survey and the media campaigns that had led up to it were seen as deeply humiliating and demeaning to queer folk. Not only did it give homophobic groups a stage to spread their hate and attack LGBTIQA+ people and their families, it also had the more subtle effect of placing the LGBTIQA+ communities in the position of petitioning to be recognized as equal. So the YES side ramped up their activism in return. Rainbow YES's and flags appeared in windows and on fences, and rainbow yarnbombs wrapped around trees and poles. Badges, pins, shirts, and patches all proclaimed their wearer's support of the LGBTQAI+ community and their love. When the final tally was in, 79 percent of Australians voted, with 62 percent of those voting yes.

# CHAPTER FIVE

# Quilting

Australians send an average of 501,000 tons of textile waste to landfill every year. This is one of the highest averages in the world. America throws away 15 million tons of textile waste while the UK throws out 300,000.

Furthermore, it's most likely that the clothes being counted in these statistics were made in third world factories by people paid a fraction of a cent per hour. Given the human and environmental impact of the manufacture and then disposal of these clothes, it's important to be responsible with your purchases and give some thought to disposing of them appropriately.

We also grow close to special items in our wardrobe—things that have shared adventures and special moments with us—and they become items we can't bear to throw away.

The growing trend of "Make Do and Mend" encourages people to spend some time to mend or upcycle their old clothes rather than simply throwing them out. Quilting, for example, is a perfect way to keep your old fabrics close while giving them new life as comforters. This way you keep the fabrics you love in your life while cutting down on waste.

A quick note on measurements: the quilt patterns are only in inches, as those are what was used in traditional quilting measurements.

Once you've finished your quilt top, head to Appendix Six on page 192 for quilting and binding instructions.

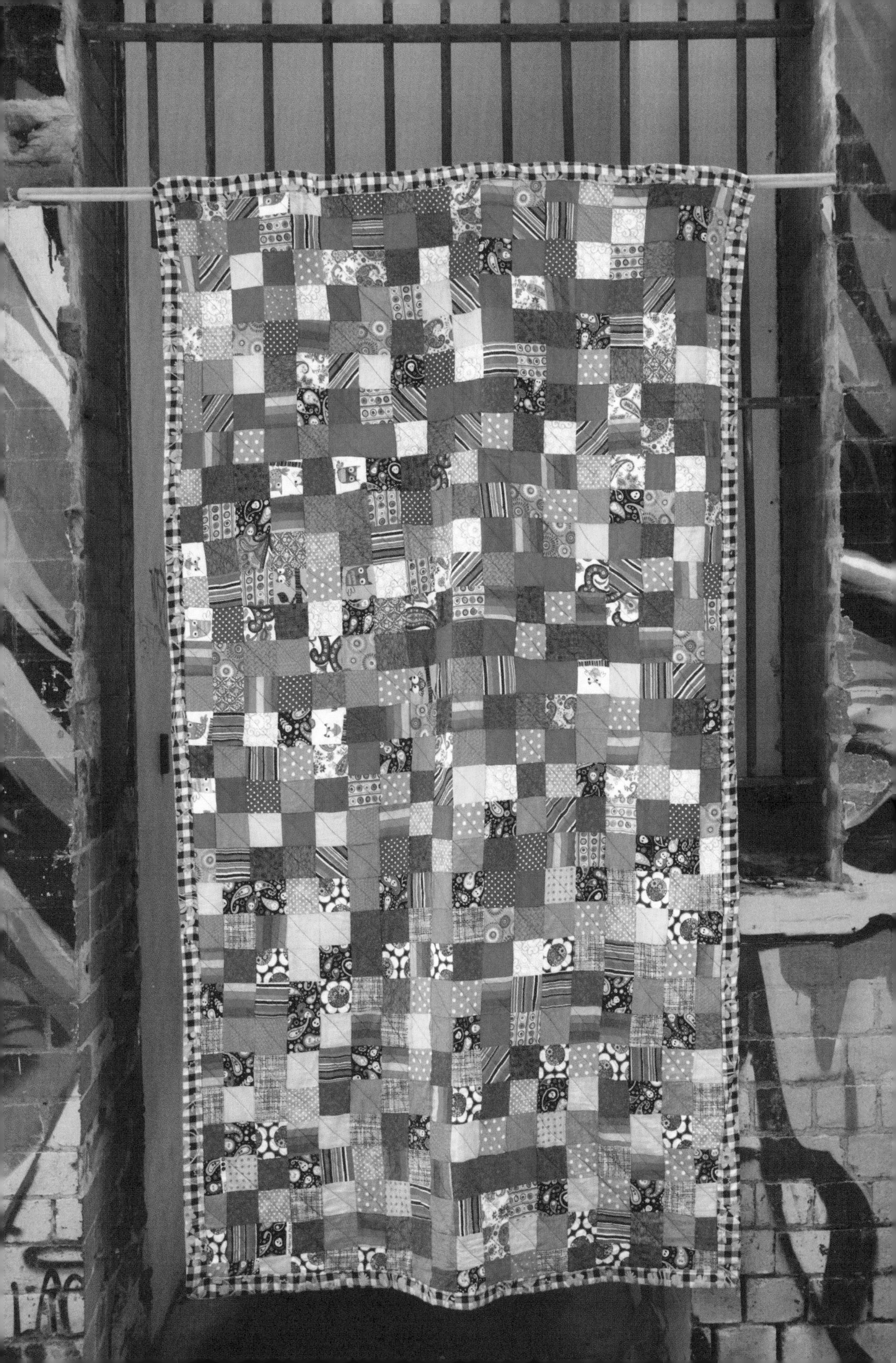

# Scrappy Quilt

## WHAT YOU'LL NEED

*Fabric*

*Wadding (such as a blanket)*

*Backing fabric
(a sheet a bit bigger than the
wadding blanket is perfect)*

*Sewing machine and thread*

*Scissors*

*Iron and ironing board*

**Not necessary but ideal**

*Cutting board*

*Rotary cutter*

*Ruler*

*Sewing machine*

If this is your first quilt, congratulations! Quilts are awesome, but be warned—they are time consuming. You might want to start with bigger fabric blocks to make it happen more quickly. Stitching a quilt out of 6 x 3-inch (15 x 7½-centimeter) patches will be much faster than one made from 1-inch (2½-centimeter) squares.

Decide on your pattern. For this quilt, I wanted to use all the left over random bits of cotton fabric I had remaining from various projects over the years. I decided simple 2½-inch (6½-centimeter) squares would look great with the riotous colors. However, this simple technique can be used with any size pieces as long as they're easy to sew together. (Stick with squares and/or rectangles for your first quilt—curves are much harder!)

I decided that I'd go with the random layout. I tried to ensure that two squares of the same fabric never ended up side by side, but was only mostly successful at that. I don't mind at all: I like that it's now a "spot the colors" style quilt where you can idly spend time searching to see where the fabric matches up. Also, don't be afraid to use all the parts of the fabric; for example, using the selvage makes an interesting little accent to the blocks.

## DIRECTIONS

1. Iron your fabric. Boring but necessary.

2. Cut out your pieces. You're going to need a lot. For this quilt, I cut 2½-inch squares.

3. Start stitching them together. The fastest way to do this is to "chain" them together into pairs. In chaining, instead of snipping the thread between sewing the pieces, you simply feed the next pair in though the machine, leaving ½-inch (1-centimeter) gap between each pair.

4. Once you have lots of pieces sewn in pairs, start stitching pairs together into quads (4s), again using the chain method.

5. Sew each of the quads together into octs (8s) and so on. Keep an eye on how you're sewing them together—you don't want to end up with one very, very long strip of your fabric, remember you're trying to create the shape of your wadding— baby blanket, single, double or queen size blanket.

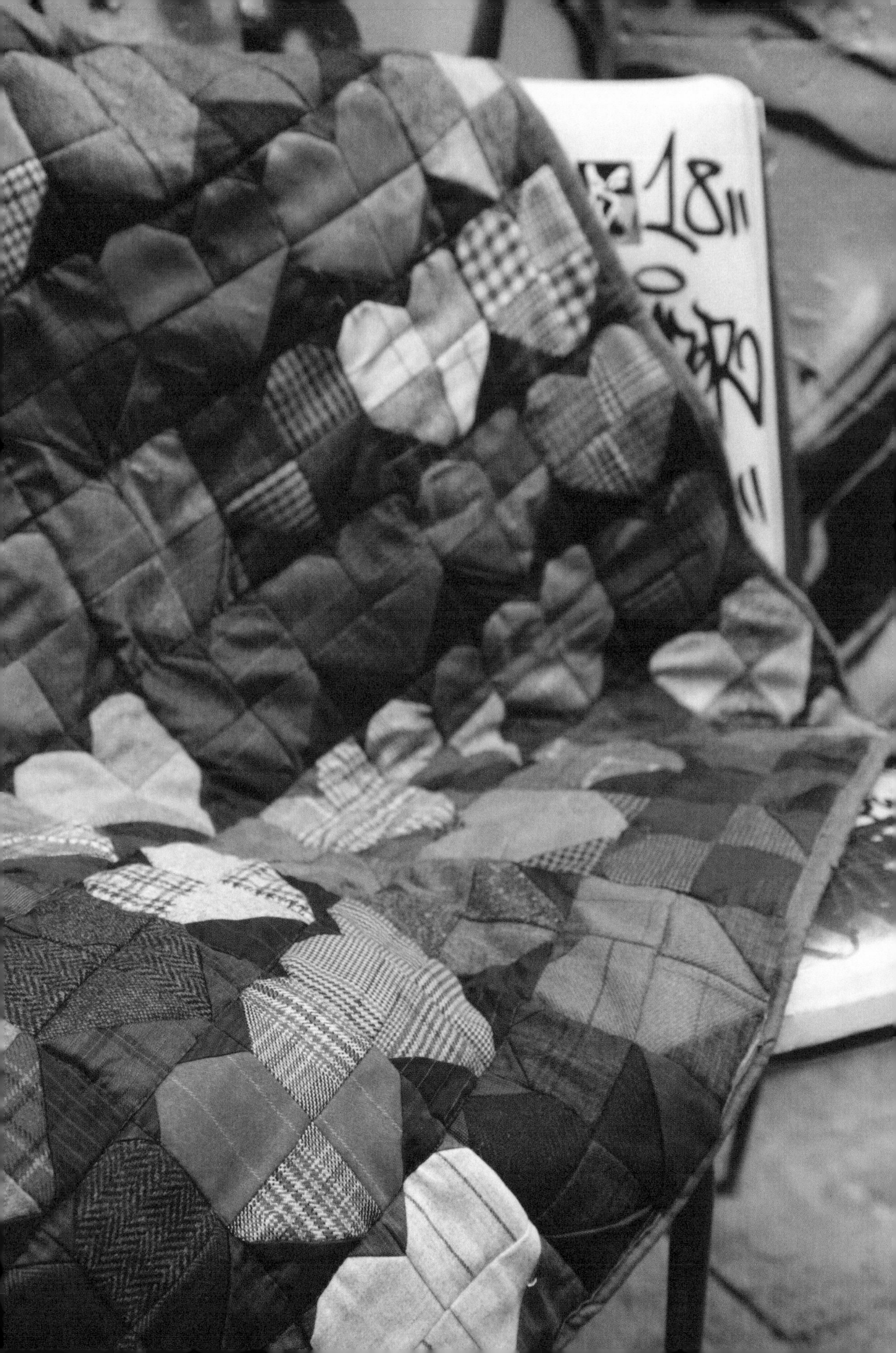

# Suit of Hearts Quilt

## WHAT YOU'LL NEED

*Suit samples or other fabric*

*Thread*

*Pins*

*Iron and ironing board*

*Sewing machine and thread*

*Cutting board*

*Ruler*

*This heart block is made up of 4 x 3-inch squares for the heart itself and 2 x 3-inch squares and 4 x 1/5-inch squares for the background to the heart.*

**Optional**
*(but will make it a lot easier)*

*Rotary cutter*

This is an historic Australian style of quilt: the Wagga Quilt. There are several types of the Wagga Quilt, but my favorites are these suiting sample quilts. In Australia during the Depression of the 1930s, housewives would ask door-to-door suit salesmen for last season's fabric swatch books. These were good quality wool and linen swatches that the women could sew into warm quilts for their families. No one quite knows where the name "Wagga Quilt" comes from, but one of the most plausible explanations was that often in the very early days of the style, the wadding for the quilt was made from Wagga brand cotton flour bags, which were milled in Wagga Wagga, New South Wales.

I emailed my local tailor to ask if they had any spare samples, and they were very happy to give me a giant bag full. The tailor told me that they hate throwing them away, but people rarely ask for them. They were very pleased I wanted to make quilts from them!

Obviously, these quilts can be made from any fabric you have, but if you like the look of the suit samples, why not email your local tailor? You never know, they might be delighted to hand them over!

There are a couple of useful things to know about using suit samples. One is that most samples have a sticker on the back that lists the manufacturer and the details of the fabric. Sometimes these come off easily and leave no residue, but sometimes the adhesive will leave a residue, which can make it difficult to sew. I feel these sticky stickers are best left on; you can either cut your pieces to avoid the stickers, or if you have to include them, you can just ignore them and sew straight through.

## DIRECTIONS

1. To make your hearts stand out, sort your fabric into lights and darks. Sort the suit samples into greys/light blues/browns and blacks/navy blues. If you're

lucky enough that your sample source has given you interesting jacket fabrics, you might sort into colors and greys/blacks/navy blues.

2. Work out how big you want your quilt to be. I've made this quilt to suit the lap rug I bought as wadding. It measures 53 inches (135 centimeters) by 42 inches (106 centimeters). The block ends up being 4½ inches (12 centimeters) square, which means I'll need 8 blocks across and 10 down—80 blocks to make my quilt. If you're making a larger quilt for a single or double bed, you'll need to measure and work out how many blocks you'll require.

3. To make the block, take one of your 3-inch background squares and fold it diagonally, pressing the folded edge firmly with your fingers to create a crease. This is "finger pressing" and it helps create a line to follow when sewing.

4. Place your newly creased 3-inch background square on top of a 3-inch heart square, right sides together. (Sometimes in suiting it's hard to tell which is which, don't worry, it doesn't matter as much as when you're using printed fabric.) Pin either side of the crease and then sew down the crease.

5. Cut away one corner of the square following the stitched line, leaving ¼-inch seam allowance.

6. Fold open and iron flat.

7. Repeat for the other bottom square of your heart.

8. For the top squares, it's a very similar process, just with the smaller 1½-inch squares. Fold diagonally and finger crease two 1½-inch squares.

9. Pin each creased square to the top corner of a 3-inch heart square with the crease sloping up and into the center.

10. Stitch along the finger crease and trim away the excess. This is called "snowballing" because if you do it to all four corners, you end up with an octagonal shape that looks a bit like a snowball.

11. Fold open and iron flat.

12. Repeat for the second top square.

13. To sew your heart together, start with the two bottom squares of the heart. Pin them together right sides facing in, ensuring both stitching lines slope down to meet at the bottom. Stitch, leaving ¼-inch seam allowance.

14. Fold open and iron flat.

15. Pin the two top squares together, right sides together, ensuring that the snowballed corners of both are at the top. Stitch together, leaving ¼-inch seam allowance.

16. Place top and bottom of the heart together, right sides together, and pin along the middle seam. Open the heart to make sure both blocks are the right way up and that you've pinned it so that you will sew along the middle seam, rather than honors sewing the top edge of the block to the bottom edge. Stitch together, leaving a ¼-inch seam allowance.

17. Fold open and iron flat.

18. Repeat until you have enough blocks for your quilt.

19. Start stitching your hearts together. The easiest way is to "chain" them together. In chaining, instead of snipping the thread between sewing the pieces, you simply feed the next pair in though the machine, leaving a ½-inch (1-centimeter) gap between each pair. When sewing the hearts together, go slowly over the hems if you're using thicker material.

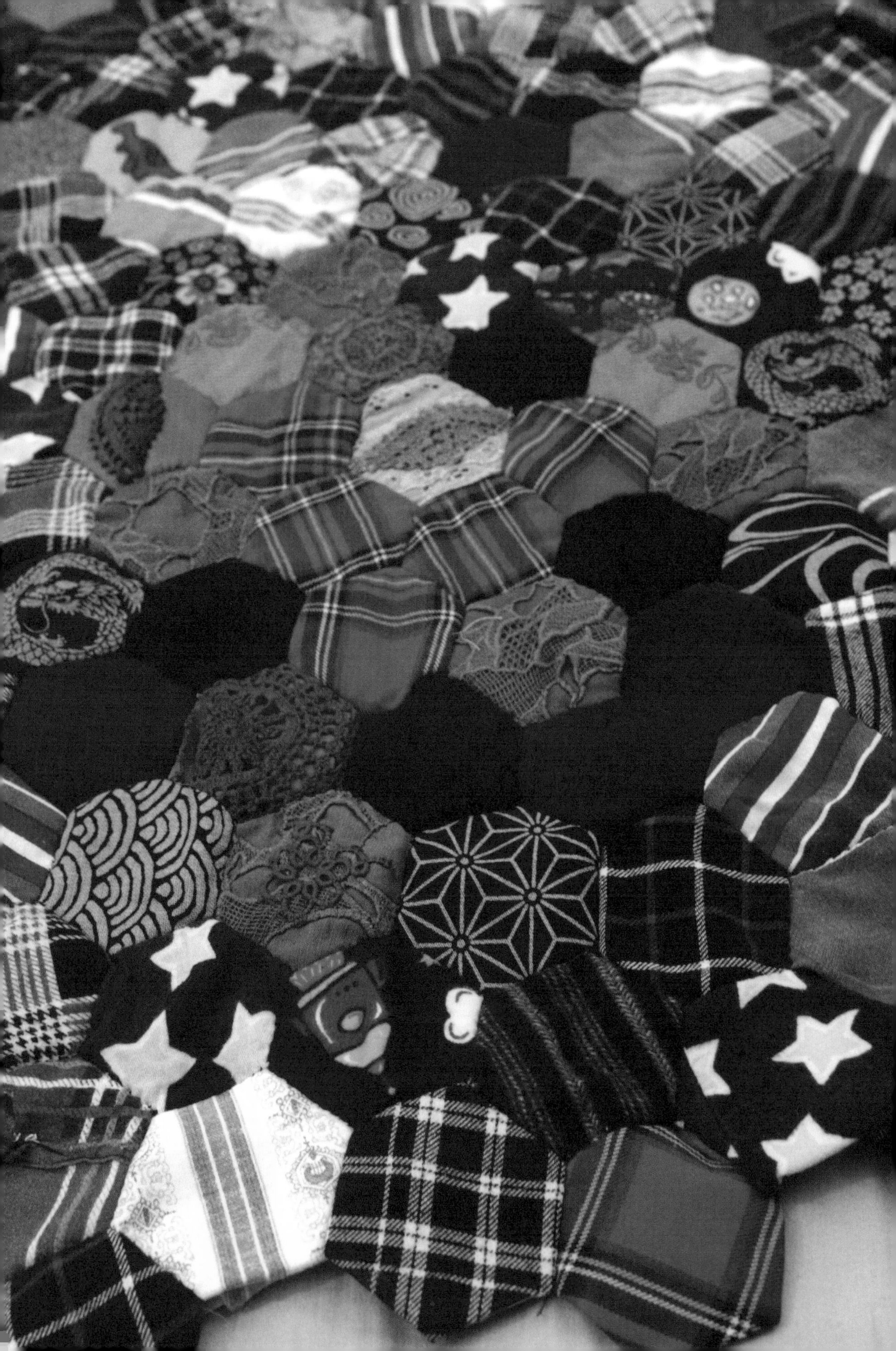

# History Hexie Quilt

## WHAT YOU'LL NEED

*Paper hexie pattern
(page 224)*

*Fabric*

*Scissors*

*Needle and thread*

*Paper clip*

*Scrap paper*

This beautiful hexagon quilt is hand sewn in the traditional English Paper Piecing style using fabric from old clothes with special meaning to you.

My hand sewn History Hexie quilt is made up of my husband's old flannelette shirts (including his first one, which he bought when he was sixteen) and fabric from my public art projects, interspersed with the occasional piece of material from my late grandmother's stash. There's also a hexie heart made from pieces of my wedding dress and my husband's suit. It is an excellent quilt; however, I'm not going to lie to you, I haven't finished it yet. This is my winter project to do on cold nights in front of the fire, the one I pick up when I have some time and put back down when I don't. It doesn't have a deadline to finish it, so it's a lovely, gentle, no pressure project. Which I haven't finished yet.

Don't let that dishearten you! If you're not keen on the hand sewing, head over to the Scrappy Quilt on page 94 and make your treasured fabrics into squares or rectangles for machine sewing.

But if you want a lovely, gentle, hand sewn project, this is beautiful. Plus, it'll be an amazing quilt full of memories and warmth by the time you're finished.

I've chosen a random pattern, but there are other ways to put hexies together, including the very old pattern Grandmother's Flower Garden. Do a quick internet search for "hexie quilt" or "hexagon quilt" to see how other people have done their hexies!

A quick note about the printing of the pattern: if you have scrap paper, use it to print your patterns, as you will need a lot of them. I've seen the back of hexie quilts from the 1800s where they've used bills, letters, and cards, and these scraps are an amazing window into their day-to-day lives.

## DIRECTIONS

1. Photocopy the hexie pattern; start with ten pages or so. Spend an evening cutting them out, maybe in front of the TV.

2. Cut your fabric about ¾ inches (2 centimeters) bigger than the paper hexie (it doesn't have to be precise). I don't mind if there's seams from the clothes in my hexies, it just shows that each piece of fabric has a history and was something else before it came to live in this quilt.

3. Place the fabric right side down and place the paper hexie in the middle.

4. Fold one edge of the fabric over the paper hexie, using a paper clip to secure it.

5. Fold the side next to the paper clip over and stitch twice across the folded fabric to hold it. It doesn't have to be neat or done with matching thread, since it won't be seen once the quilt is done.

6. Continue to fold and stitch each corner until you finish your hexie.

7. Repeat steps 2 to 6.

8. A lot.

9. Now to stitch hexies together. With the right sides of the hexies together and edges lined up, start by securing a couple of firm stitches (or a knot) in the corner. Whip stitch all the way down one side. The closer and smaller the stitches, the more inconspicuous from the front. Just catch the edges and not the paper inside. Finish with a couple of stitches in the corner to secure.

10. Grab another hexie and repeat step 9.

11. And again.

12. And again.

13. And then some more.

14. It's nice to see progress when you're working on a big project, so when I have seven hexies, I stitch them into a "flower." You can use the same colors to make your flower stand out, or you can just use random hexies. For my hexie quilt, I've gone mostly random but tried to make sure no two hexies of the same material touched. I've been mostly successful at this.

15. Keep going until your quilt top is big enough. Remember to spread it out and measure it occasionally so you don't end up with a very long, very thin quilt top or a quilt with an extra bulge of hexies on one side.

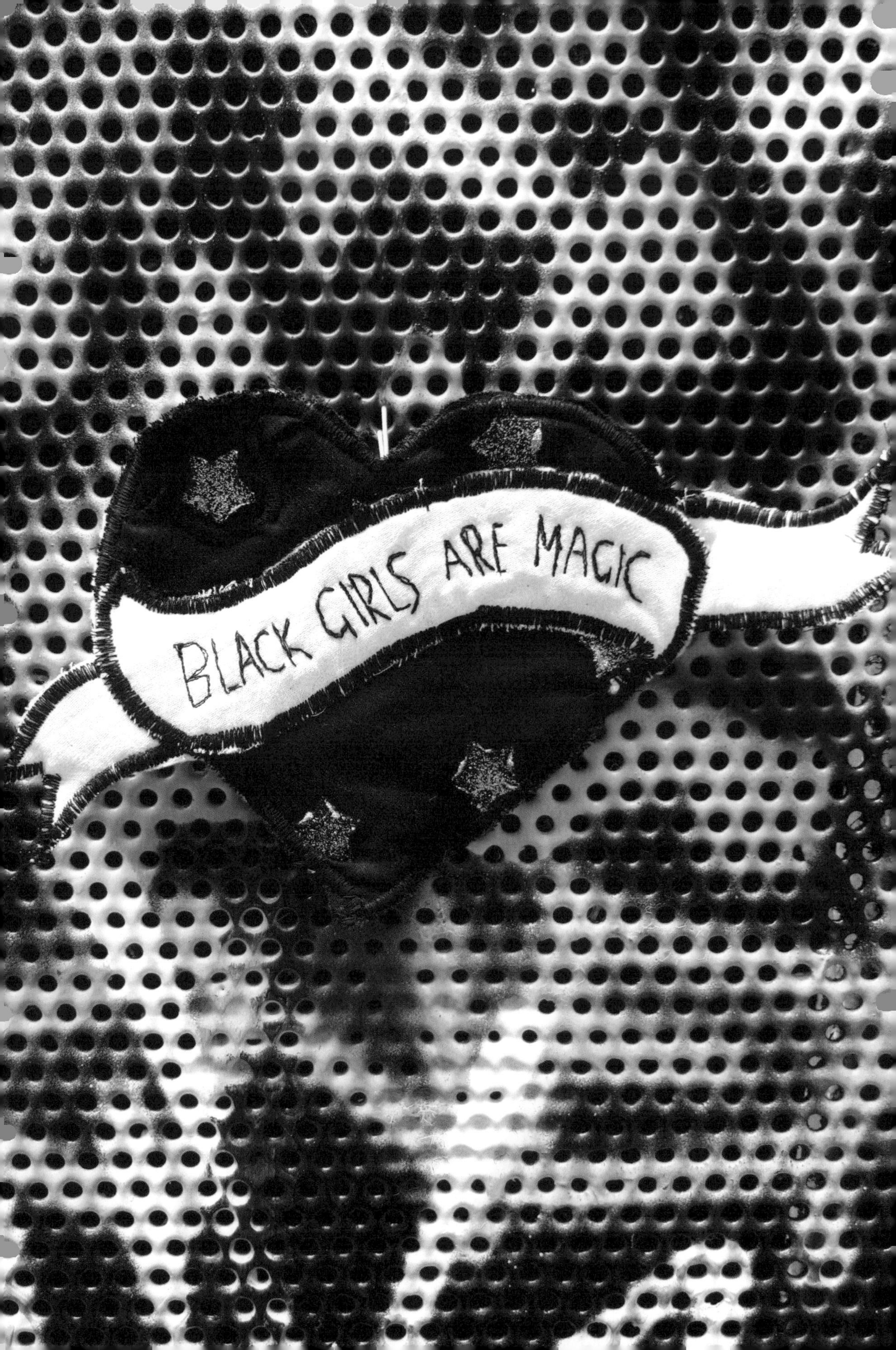
BLACK GIRLS ARE MAGIC

# Quilted Patches

## WHAT YOU'LL NEED

*Pattern (page 225)*

*Fabric for the heart and banner (the fabric for the "Black Girls are Magic" heart was first potato stamped with glittery stars; see page 137 for the potato stamp project)*

*Backing fabric*

*Wadding
(I used a baby's blanket bought from a charity store)*

*Sewing machine and thread*

*Scissors*

*Pins*

These patches are fun, quick to do, and totally customizable for any cause. They're quick to whip up, and you don't even need a seam allowance. There's no need to hem them because the appliqué stitching at the edge will keep them from fraying. This project is designed to be a little messy, so don't be afraid to have some threads hanging out! Once finished, these can be stitched to banners, clothing, or bags or else displayed as is.

Each patch is made up of three layers: fabric, wadding and a backing fabric so they have a little bit of "puff" to them.

This old school heart and ribbon can be customized with different fabric choices for the heart, and any slogans can be hand or machine stitched on the ribbon.

You can also use the ribbon part of the pattern with the face either up or down depending on which way you want it to flow. The "Love is Love" heart uses the pattern as is on the fabric, and the "Black Girls are Magic" heart uses the pattern reversed.

If you want to design your own symbol,
follow the second set of instructions below.

## DIRECTIONS

1. Photocopy the pattern and cut out each shape.

2. Each piece of your pattern needs to be cut three times: one each from the top fabric, the wadding, and the backing fabric. If your pattern has layers (such as the ends of the ribbon which go under the heart in the pattern provided), you'll need to cut some extra length to be able to sew it together. (See the seam allowance at the end of the ribbons on the pattern.)

3. Pin together each of the three layers of each shape. Once they're pinned together, feel free to trim the wadding/backing fabric if they're peeking out too much from the front fabric.

4. Set your machine to "Satin Stitch." Some machines have this as a specific setting, otherwise set it to a wide zig zag with a longer stitch width and a smaller stitch length. This should give you a nice tight zigzag with barely any fabric showing through the stitch. Try it out on a scrap piece of fabric until you're happy with the stitching. Once you have a good satin stitch sorted, stitch around the edge of both ribbon ends. Try not to run off the edge of the fabric with your stitches, instead think of it as tracing around just inside the edge. It can be tricky to feed the smaller items through the sewing machine when there's not a lot of material to grasp behind the needle. If this is the case, you can lift the sewing foot and needle and shift the fabric just a little bit back, then replace the foot and keep sewing. You might need to lift the foot and needle a couple of times until there's enough material behind that you can grasp to be able to help guide the fabric through. Be patient and go slowly, it'll work.

5. Place the ribbon ends underneath the heart and pin them in the right spot.

6. Satin stitch around the heart, making sure to incorporate the ribbon ends.

7. Satin stitch the edge of the main ribbon separately from the heart.

8. Now it's time for the slogan. You can use a special fabric pen (these come in two kinds: either with ink that will fade after 24 hours or that can be wiped away with a damp cloth), you can lightly pencil it in, or you can just go freehand with the stitching. If you haven't machine stitched words before, test your skills on a scrap piece of fabric. A few tips: a short stitch length will help with the curves, using the hand wheel rather than the foot pedal can help with forming the letters, and you can go over and over the lines to thicken them. Feel free to hand stitch the slogan if you prefer, or cut out letters from felt and stitch them on (see the Pennant project on page 83 for this style of lettering).

9. Once your slogan is finished, pin your ribbon across the heart and satin stitch around the edge.

10. Trim any excess threads away, and you're done!

11. If you want to hang your new patch up, hand stitch a small loop of ribbon to the back. The wadding and quilting should make it firm enough to hang without wilting.

## DESIGNING YOUR OWN PATCH

Of course, your patch doesn't have to be in the shape of a heart and ribbon. If you're not comfortable hand drawing a different shape or symbol, then a quick internet search should bring up what you're looking for. Try searching for your symbol name and the term "clip art" or "drawing." If you're using a symbol other than the heart and ribbon shape provided, make sure it's at least 4 inches (10 centimeters) in width so it's not too tricky to make. The skull was part of a barter quilt I made for my tattooist (see the full quilt in the Barter chapter, page 168) I found a clip art skull I liked on the internet and traced it out (see the instructions on the Embroidery on Reclaimed Fabric project on page 74). I stitched it in exactly the same way as the old school heart: I cut out backing fabric and wadding in the same shape, pinned the three layers together, and satin stitched around the edge. Then I cut out eye shapes and satin stitched them on and finally did a single line of stitching to draw the teeth. To attach it to my quilt, I simply satin stitched around the edge again.

## Black Girls are Magic

Black Girls are Magic (also Black Girl Magic) is a movement on social media which celebrates the beauty, power, and resilience of black women. It was popularized by CaShawn Thompson in 2013 to counteract the negativity and stereotypes that society places on black women and to celebrate their achievements. It is a declaration of pride among black girls and women which has become a worldwide movement.

#blackgirlsaremagic, #blackgirlmagic

# DIY Quilt Block

Now you know how to stitch straight squares, squares with snowballed corners, and squares comprised of two triangles, you can design any kind of symbol into a block! Grab yourself a piece of gridded paper and try some out. Here's a little inspiration, but feel free to come up with your own designs. You can use the same block over and over or combine different blocks to be incorporated into banners, stitched onto clothing, or even sewn into an actual quilt.

If you need more inspiration for how to combine simple shapes to make more complex images, try an internet search with the name of your symbol (for instance "skull quilt") to see how other people are making the block you want to create.

When designing your blocks, remember that symbols can benefit from a simple border of squares around them to visually separate them from their neighbors.

You can also use the Quilted Patches technique (page 106) to appliqué images and letters to your quilt.

If you're making a quilt, you'll need to figure out how many blocks you'll need. There are two ways to do this. The first is with math. Divide the width of your desired quilt by the width of your quilt block. That's how many blocks you'll need for each row. Then divide the length of your desired quilt by the length of your block to find out how many rows you'll need.

The other way is simply lay out your blocks on your wadding in a single row to find how many blocks you need to make a row. Then lay them out down your wadding to find how many rows you'll need.

Either way you do it, remember to add in the width of any borders you plan to include.

Once your quilt is sewn together, follow the instructions for Quilting and Binding in Appendix Six.

# CHAPTER SIX

# Visible Mending

During the Second World War the British Government released a pamphlet titled "Make Do and Mend" which was aimed at encouraging people to repair their clothes rather than replacing them with new ones. This then freed up manufacturing plants and labor to produce fabric for the war effort.

This Make Do and Mend mentality has had a resurgence over the last ten years, and it's heartwarming that all over the world people are choosing to prolong the life of their clothes rather than just toss them out.

There are many beautiful things about patching your old clothes. It's environmentally friendly, it's economical, and it also honors the work of the person who originally sewed them. Whether you bought it from a store or from a maker, whether someone among your family or friends made it or you sewed it yourself, mending an item prolongs its life, and you get to wear the clothes you love for longer.

If you use visible mending, a technique wherein you deliberately keep the repairs obvious, you can literally wear the history of the garment proudly on your sleeve. You can read the story of the garment in its wear and tear, its patches and mends.

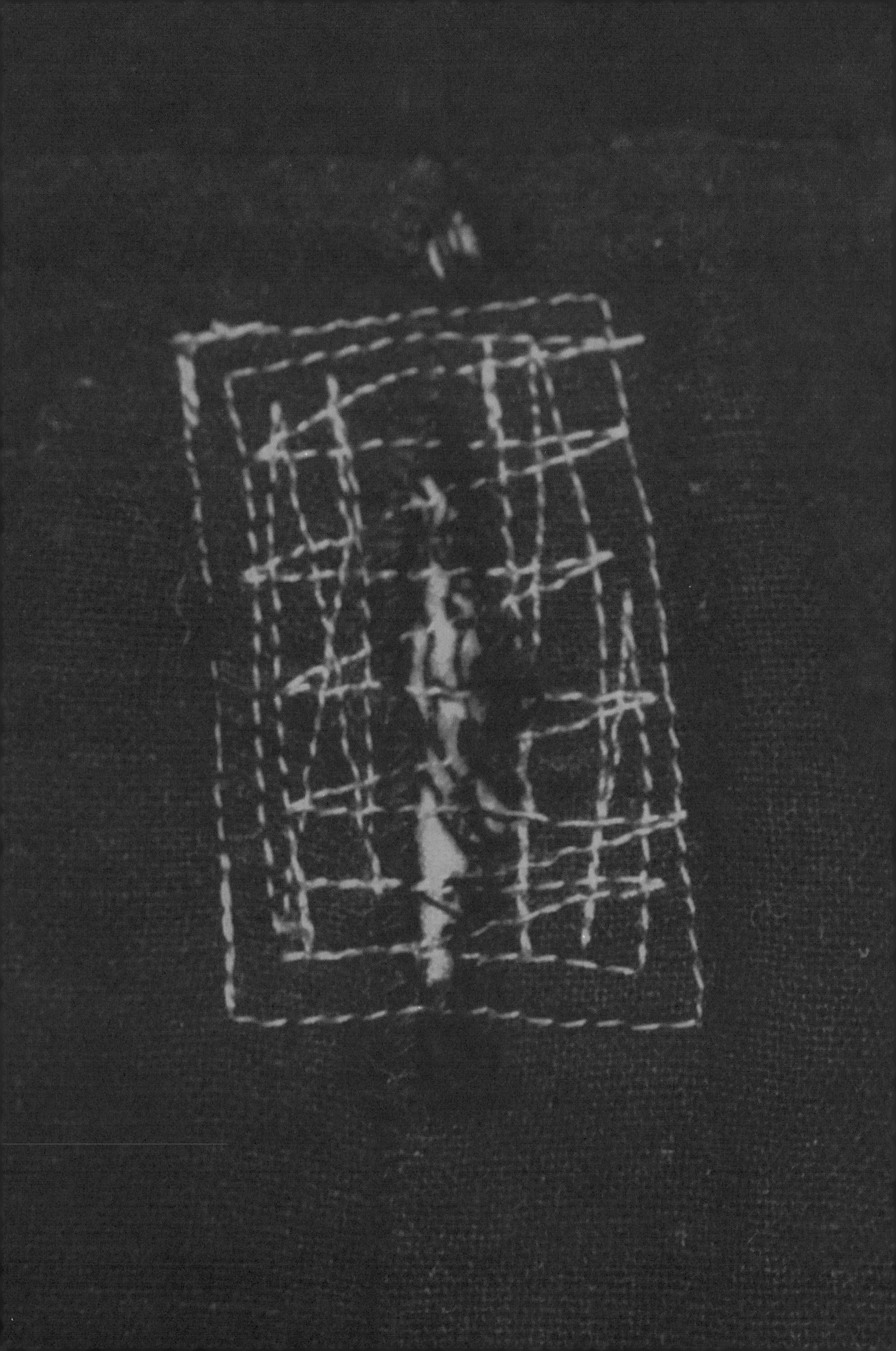

# Simple Visible Mending

## WHAT YOU'LL NEED

*Non-stretch and strong material for the underneath patch (denim, corduroy, thick cotton, or other)*

*Needle or sewing machine and thread*

*Scissors*

*Pins*

*Something with a hole in it*

When my favorite jeans were starting to tear through a few years ago, I went to my sister and asked her how best to patch them. She taught me the method she uses, which was taught to her by our late grandmother. I love the family history in the knowledge that I am patching my jeans the same way my sister does, which is the same way my mum does and my grandmother did. This is the method I get to pass onto you.

There are two approaches to this simple mending. With one, the patch you use underneath the hole is visible, and with the other, you put a final patch on top of the hole.

---

## UNDERNEATH PATCH

### DIRECTIONS

1. Cut a patch from contrasting fabric, 1 inch (2 centimeters) bigger than the hole.

2. Turn the clothing inside out and position the underneath patch against the hole.

3. Pin the patch down, tucking ¼ inch (½ centimeter) underneath for the hem.

4. Stitch around the edge of the patch with a straight stitch.

5. Turn the clothing right side out again and stitch zig zags across the hole several times. This strengthens the holey/fragile fabric by attaching it to the tougher material behind it.

6. Wear your newly patched clothing with pride.

## TOP PATCH

If you prefer the look of a single top patch without the stitching all over it, or if the clothing gets a lot of wear and you think it might benefit from an extra patch for more strength, this method works great.

## WHAT YOU'LL NEED

*Non-stretch and strong
material for the underneath
patch (denim, corduroy,
thick cotton, or other)*

*Needle or sewing machine
and thread*

*Scissors*

*Pins*

*Something with a hole in it*

*Extra fabric for the top
patch*

## DIRECTIONS

1. Follow the Underneath Patch instructions above from steps 1 through 5.

2. Once the underneath patch is sewn firmly, cut another patch from contrasting fabric and pin on top of the hole, again tucking ¼ inch (½ centimeter) underneath for the hem

3. Stitch around the edge. You can use a machine or stitch by hand. As the patch in the photo is partly on top of a pocket in the jeans, I went with hand stitching so I could make sure I wasn't stitching through the pocket and thus rendering it useless.

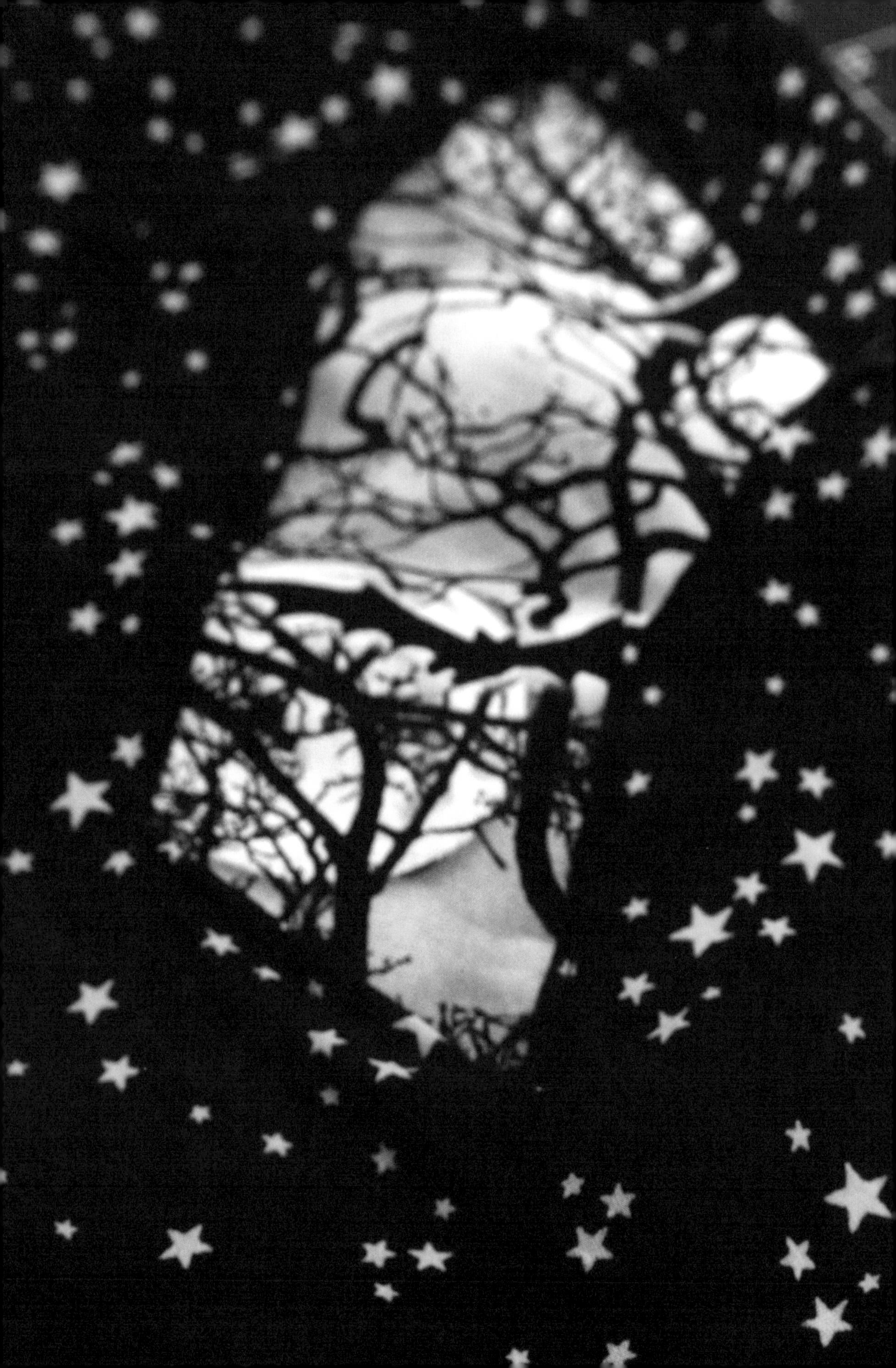

# Larger Holes

**WHAT YOU'LL NEED**

*Something with a hole in it*

*Pins*

*Needle or sewing machine and thread*

*Contrasting fabric*

This is a shirt I found at a charity shop with a large rip in the elbow. I didn't leave it where I found it because I knew I could mend it and make it even better.

When you embark on this type of mending, be aware that if the tear is an old one, the fabric might be a little stretched and could be a little tricky to pin flat to the patch. Persist, it'll work. Eventually.

## DIRECTIONS

1. First, iron the garment. I'm not a fan of ironing, but sometimes it's necessary. Ironing the hole and the fabric around it will help you understand the size and shape of the hole.

2. Cut a patch from contrasting fabric, 1 inch (2 centimeters) bigger than the hole.

3. Pin ½ inch (1½ centimeters) around the entire patch and hem.

4. Position the patch underneath the hole to your liking; try to ensure that the garment lies as flat as possible.

5. Pin the patch to the fabric, folding ¼ inch (½ centimeters) of the edge of the hole underneath for a hem.

6. Once it's pinned, try the garment on (very carefully!) to make sure you've pinned it flat.

7. Stitch around the edge of the hole with a straight stitch or use satin stitch, whichever you prefer.

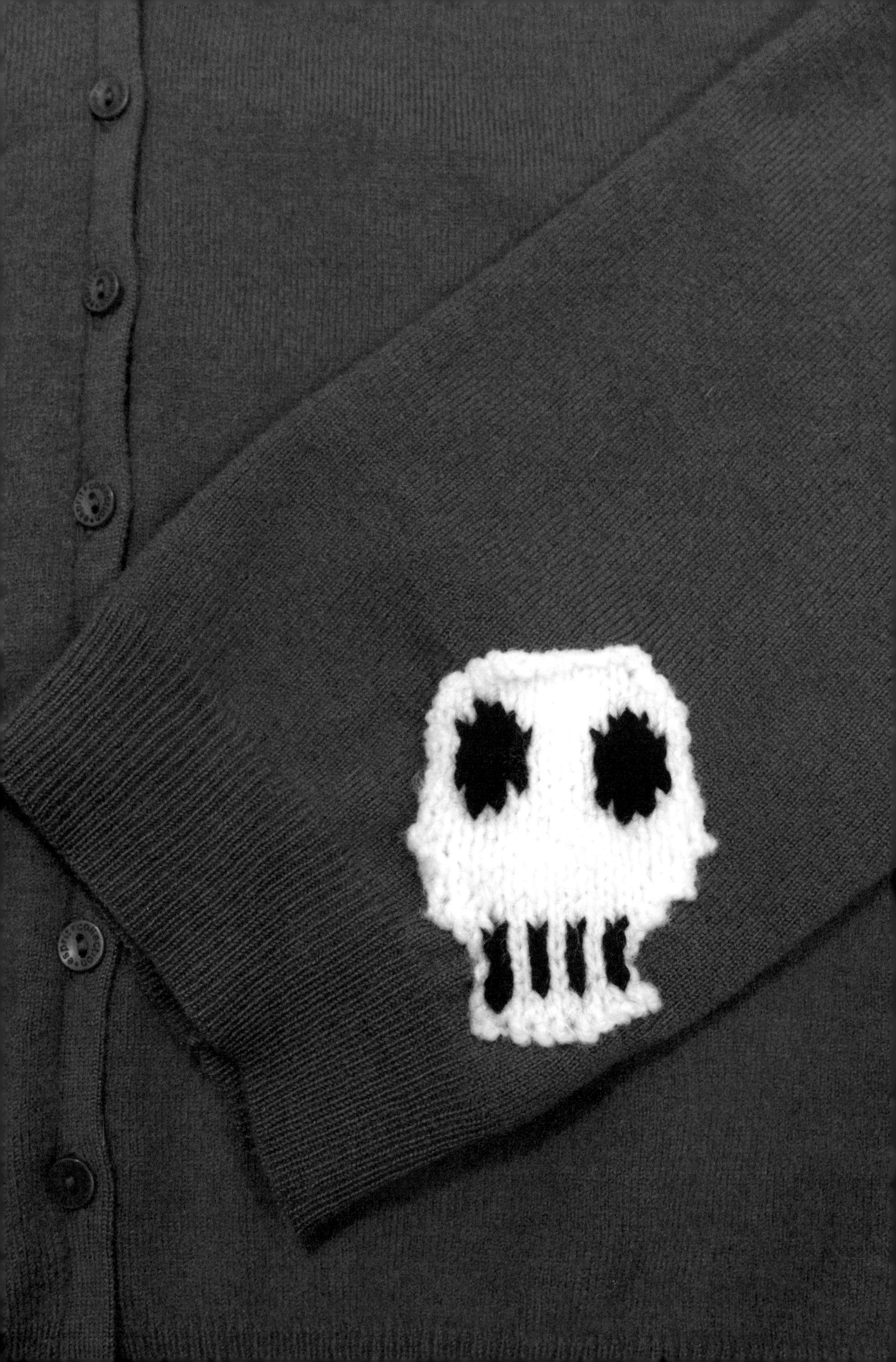

# Mending Knitted Things

*Something knitted
with a hole in it*

*A darning or yarn needle*

*Yarn of a contrasting
color to the garment but
around the same thickness
as the yarn the garment is
knitted with*

There are several ways to mend knitted fabric. I'm going to show you the simplest two. Firstly, mending the hole itself by darning will keep the garment from unravelling further, and then you can knit a patch to go on top.

## DARNING

Darning is a method of weaving yarn in and out through the existing stitches to bridge the hole. It's important that you don't pull the stitches tight to attempt to close up the hole, as this will pucker the fabric. Darning is about weaving new fabric into the existing hole. You can see another example of darning on one of my favorite cardigans, underneath the felt badge on page 160.

1. First you need to create a series of horizontal lines of stitching. If the hole you're patching is small, begin stitching around 3/8 inch (1 centimeter) away from the hole and then continue the same distance past the hole on the other side. If the hole is larger, you'll need to expand this distance. Stitch a single row with a simple running stitch woven in and out of the existing knitted stitches where possible.

2. When you get to the end of the row, begin on the second row heading back the way you came. Don't pull the end of the row tight, instead leave a little loose loop to allow for stretching of the fabric. Stagger your second row of running stitch to the first. Space rows as closely as possible for maximum strength (the stitching is spaced out a little more in the photos to show detail).

3. Continue your horizontal rows of running stitch until you are 3/8 inch (1 centimeter), or whatever your measurement is, past the end of the hole. Weave in the end of your yarn and snip.

4. Now for the vertical row. Repeat steps 1 to 3 vertically. In the photos, I've changed color to show the detail properly; I have used this two-tone darning in the past as well, and I love the effect! If you have any unravelled knitting stitches, try to catch them in your stitching at this point.

5. This style of darning doesn't stretch out a lot, so if it's important to you that the knit remains stretchy, then darn the second row at a 45 degree angle to the first.

# Knitted Patches

## WHAT YOU'LL NEED

*Knitting needles
(I like to use US 2/metric
2.5mm/UK 12)*

*13 feet (6 meters)
of black yarn and 6½ feet
(4 meters) of white yarn
(sports weight/8 ply)*

*Sewing needle*

*White thread*

Once you've darned the hole, or if it's small and you're not worried about it unravelling further, you can knit a shape to stitch on top of it. I've created this small skull pattern, for which you can find the pattern grid on page 226. You can also use the knitted heart pattern from page 40, or you can design your own on the empty grid on page 214. If you know how to increase and decrease in knitting and how to change colors while knitting, you're all set to create your own shapes and symbols. If you don't, check out the appendices on knitting on page 179 to learn everything you need to know.

## DIRECTIONS

✦ Cast on 9 stitches in white

✦ Row 1: knit all white

✦ Row 2 to 5: knit 1 white, 1 black, repeat to end of row

✦ Row 6: knit all white

✦ Row 7 to 9: increase at start, knit all white, increase at end

- ✦ Row 10 to 12: knit all white

- ✦ Row 13: knit 3 white, 2 black, 5 white, 2 black, 3 white

- ✦ Row 14 to 16: knit 2 white, 4 black, 3 white, 4 black, 2 white

- ✦ Row 17: knit 3 white, 2 black, 5 white, 2 black, 3 white

- ✦ Row 18: knit 3 white, 2 black, 5 white, 2 black, 3 white

- ✦ Row 19: knit all white

- ✦ Row 20 to 22: decrease at start, knit all white, decrease at end

- ✦ Cast off and weave in ends

- ✦ Pin to garment and stitch around the edge.

# CHAPTER SEVEN

# Stamps and Stencils

These next few crafts are often overlooked and omitted from an activist's arsenal. Occasionally their legitimacy as crafts is questioned, but if you look at any crafting book from the '70s and '80s, you'll find loads of stamping and stenciling techniques to decorate rooms, furniture, walls, and even clothes. So come with me to reclaim some awesome old crafts and convert them to your favorite cause.

RIOTS
NOT
DIETS

# Street Stencils

WHAT YOU'LL NEED

## WHAT YOU'LL NEED

*Pattern (page 227)*

*Thin cardboard or thin plastic (I used the side of a cereal box)[1]*

*Pencil*

*Craft knife/scalpel*

*Cutting board*

*Wide tape (often people use painters or masking tape, but any wide tape should be fine)*

*Spray paint in a contrasting color to the intended location of your piece*

Street art stencils can be quite intricate and use a lot of colors and layers, but at its most basic, stenciling is really very easy. Once you've conquered this simple, single color stencil technique, you can challenge yourself by creating more detailed stencils. When you're feeling confident, do a quick search online for "two color (or three, or four) street art stencil" to see the kinds of things you can achieve. In the meantime, my advice is to start simple with this single color slogan stencil.

## DIRECTIONS

1. Decide on your slogan. If this is your first stencil, my advice is the fewer words. the better!

2. Decide on a font. Remember that as stencil letters are cut out, you need to leave a strip or tab between the inside and the outside of the letters to hold the floating sections of the letters in place. For instance, the letter O will require tabs from the outside of the letter to the oval inside the letter.

3. When planning your stencil, remember to leave about a 1½-inch (4-centimeter) space between the end of the letters and the edge of the cardboard. This helps protect against "overspray," where the paint goes over the edge of the cardboard and leaves a little frame of paint around the piece.

4. If you're drawing the letters freehand, draw them straight onto your cardboard or plastic and skip to step

5. Print out your slogan and place it on your cardboard or plastic. Trace around each letter with a pencil, pressing hard to imprint the pattern into the stencil material.

[1] A plastic stencil will last longer than a cardboard one, so which material you should choose depends on how many times you want to use it.

6. Remove your paper and lightly color over the imprints with your pencil. The parts exposed to the pencil will contrast with the areas indented by the pattern.

7. Cut the letters carefully out of the cardboard, making your stencil. If you break the stencil anywhere or cut where you don't mean to, it's easily fixed. Place a piece of tape across the break/cut and try again. Cut away the excess tape.

8. Stick the stencil to the wall with thick tape, making sure to lay it as flat as possible.

9. Shake your spray can and spray over the stencil, making sure you are spraying directly onto the stencil and not at an angle (which will allow the paint to get under the stencil).

10. Remove your stencil carefully as the paint will be wet on top of the stencil. If the edges of the letters are a little fuzzy, that's because the stencil isn't sitting flat against the wall. Try taping it flatter to the wall for the next spray, or even finding a stick and pressing against the stencil as you spray.

## Riots Not Diets

Body image is a huge problem. On every street corner, in every publication, and on almost every website there is advertising for every product imaginable, and they all use thin, young, able-bodied and mostly white models to promote them. The Body Positive Movement pushes back against this, encouraging people to embrace their bodies no matter their perceived "flaws" and focuses on building self-esteem through improving self-image.

Sometimes activist slogans are very serious, and sometimes they are tongue-in-cheek. "Riots Not Diets" is not meant to be deadpan, it's a cheeky jest.

#bodypositivity #bodyposi #effyourbeautystandards

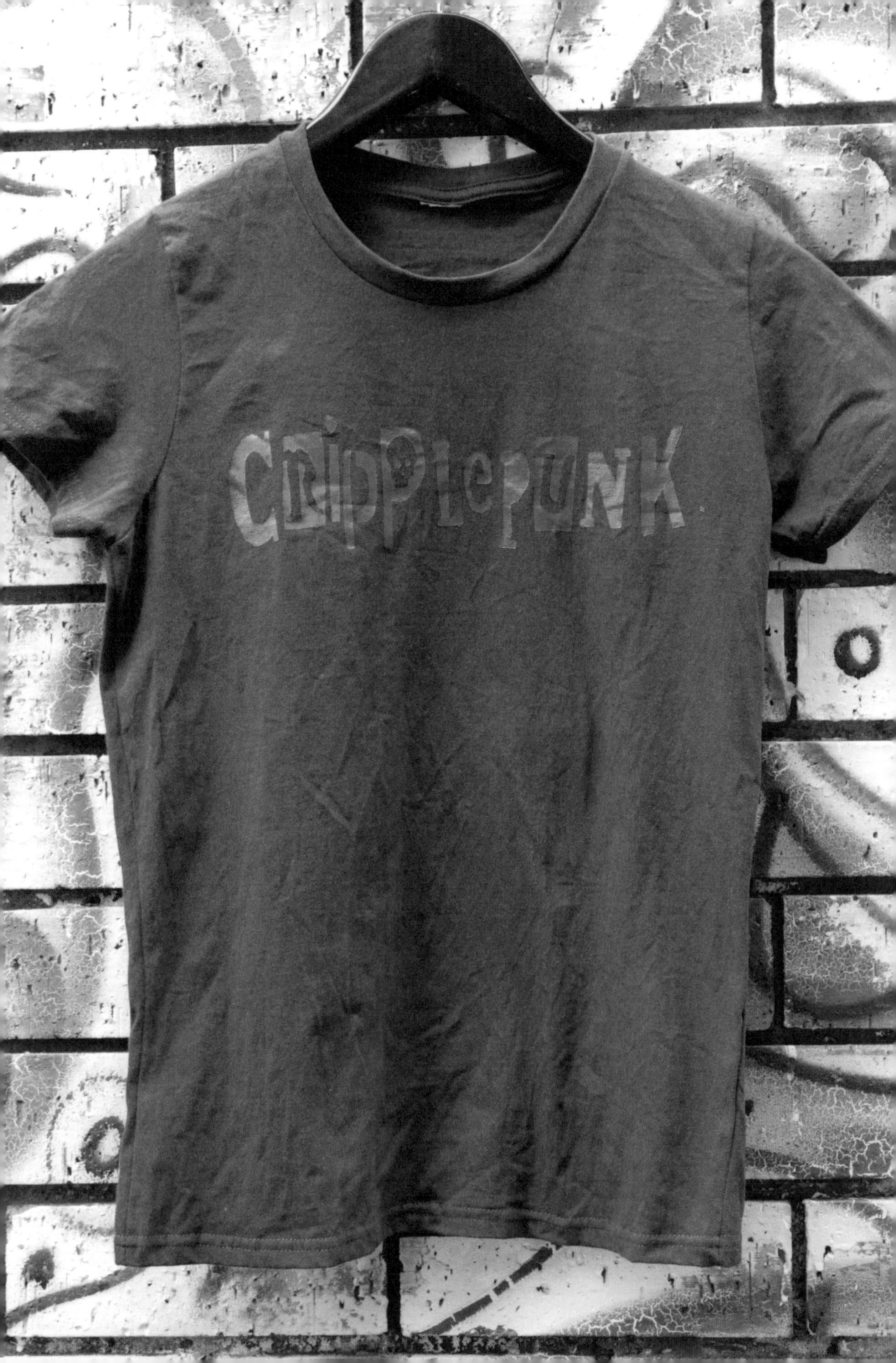
CRIPPLEPUNK

# T-shirt Stenciling

## WHAT YOU'LL NEED

*Pattern (page 228)*

*T-shirt (or other fabric)*

*Paper*

*Glue stick
(the stationary/office kind of
glue stick is fine, you don't
need to buy fancy fabric
glue sticks for this)*

*Fabric paint*

*Foam brush/foam roller/
paint brush/your finger*

*Scissors/craft knife*

**Optional**

*a pin*

In the 1960s, T-shirts started being screen printed with slogans and symbols for art and protest purposes. Although you can now upload a design and have T-shirts printed by various companies via the web, not everyone has access to the internet or can afford the costs involved. Instead, printing your own unique old school T-shirt with this technique is very simple, cheap, and fun.

Of course, you don't have to stick to just T-shirts. You can also stencil smaller pieces of fabric to make into patches or larger pieces to make into banners and pennants.

The best thing to use for this project is fabric paint. I have seen spray paint used, however, the paint hardens as it dries, so you end up with a hard, solid design on soft, bendy fabric, which can be uncomfortable and will eventually crack. Very punk, but maybe not what you're looking for.

The "CRIPPLEPUNK" pattern can be found on page 228, or you can print or draw your own. If you're making a design for a T-shirt, try to stick to an image the size of a piece of 8½" by 11" (or A4) paper or smaller. Otherwise it might not end up fitting on your shirt.

## DIRECTIONS

1. Print, photocopy, or draw your image on your stencil and cut it out. You can use scissors, but I like to use a craft knife for precision.

2. If your fabric is very wrinkled, iron it.

3. Flip your stencil over and place it on another piece of scrap paper.

4. Carefully apply the glue stick, making sure to get right to the edges of the letters. I find this easiest if I glue over the spaces in the stencil too.

5. Place your fabric onto the stencil and press down firmly, paying attention to small corners and edges to make sure they're pressed down well. Make sure there's no globs of glue showing through the letters. Anywhere there is a glob of glue, the paint won't be able to get to the fabric.

6. If you're stenciling a T-shirt or something else with another layer of fabric behind it (a bag, a pillow case) be sure to place more scrap paper between the layers in case the paint bleeds through the material onto the second layer (the back of the T-shirt, bag, or pillowcase).

7. Apply the paint. My preferred method is with a foam brush, but you can use whatever you like; however, paint brushes and fingers will give you a thicker layer of paint. When painting, be careful to brush from the outside of the letter towards the middle so that you don't accidentally push the paper back away from the design and allow the paint to bleed underneath. Do this step as quickly as you can, because you want to be able to take the stencil back off the fabric before the glue completely dries.

8. Remove the stencil. To remove any small parts of the stencil (like the skull in the letter "P"), carefully use a pin or the point of your craft knife to slide under the paper and lift it off the fabric.

9. Leave overnight to allow the paint to dry.

10. Some fabric paint requires ironing to make it permanent, while some just requires a few days drying time. Be sure to follow the instructions for your paint so your design won't wash away.

## Cripple Punk

Cripple Punk (or CPunk for those who are uncomfortable with the word "cripple") is a positivity and support movement for people with physical disabilities. It was started in 2014 by Tyler, a young disabled person on Tumblr. In the Cripple Punk manifesto, Tyler writes "Cripple Punk rejects the 'good cripple' mythos. Cripple Punk is here for the bitter cripple, the uninspirational cripple, the smoking cripple, the drinking cripple, the addict cripple, the cripple who hasn't 'tried everything' … Cripple Punk rejects pity, inspiration porn, and all other forms of ableism."[1]

Cripple Punk rejects the notion that disabled people are always "trying to get better" in order to retake their place in "normal" society. Cripple Punk demands the right of disabled people to set their own limits free from ableist assumptions and value judgements.

#cripplepunk #cpunk

1 Disgaybled. "What are the principles of cripple punk? Are there any rules?," *Crpl-pnk*, 2015. http://crpl-pnk.tumblr.com/post/104872173804/what-are-the-principles-of-cripple-punk-are-there. (Accessed March 2018.)

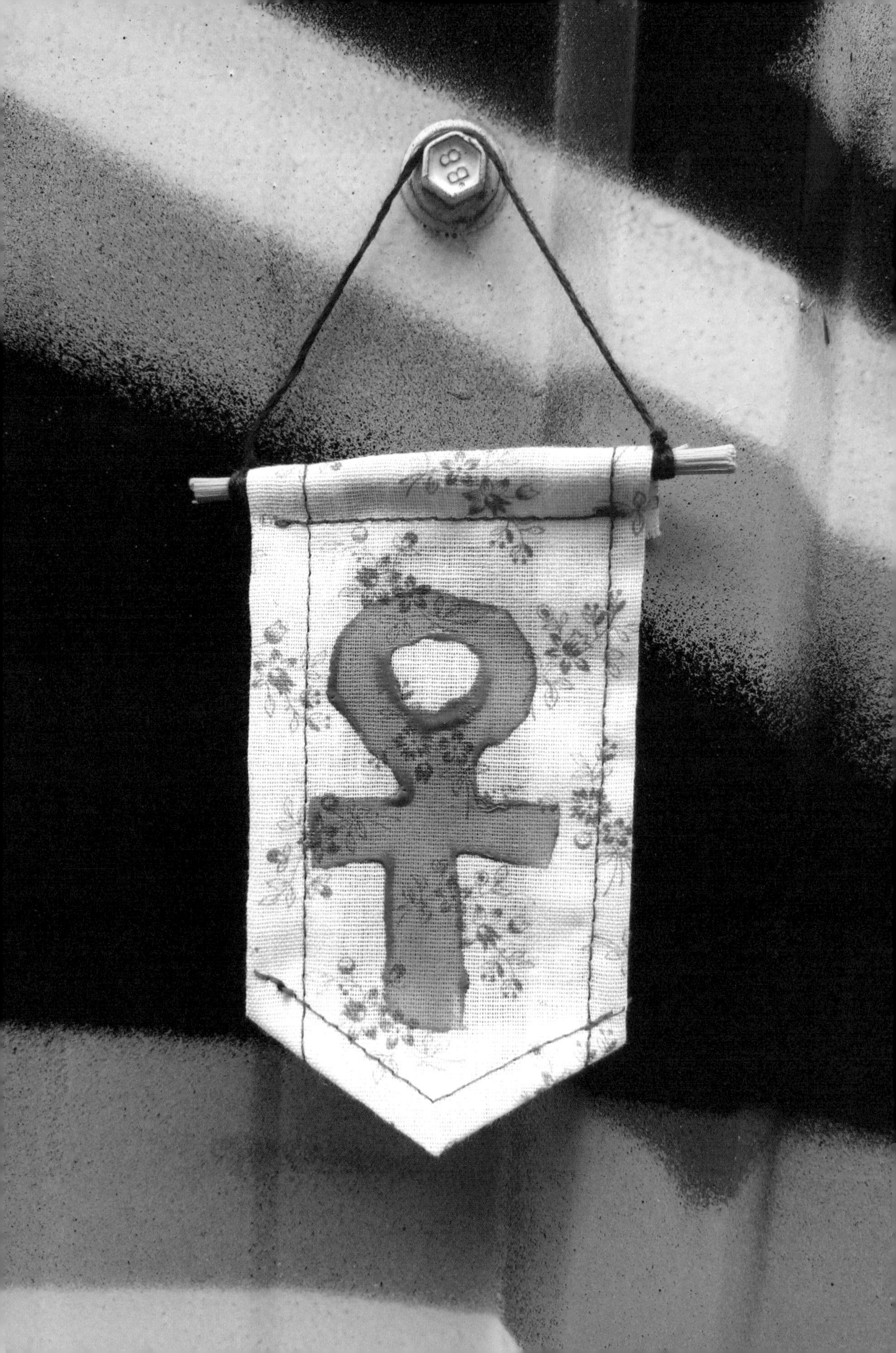

# Potato Stamp

*A big potato*

*A sharp pencil*

*A sharp knife*

*Acrylic or fabric paint*

*Paper, cards, or fabric*

**Optional**

*cookie cutter*

*Paint brush or small paint roller*

You may have made potato stamps in primary school, but it's time to revisit them with an activist's frame of mind! They're cheap and simple to make and easy to use, and they make it super quick to repeat an image. You can use fabric paint to stamp on material or ordinary acrylic paint to apply your newly minted symbol on paper, cards, or anything else.

The easiest way to make a potato stamp is to use a cookie cutter. However, you can also freehand it if you'd prefer (or if they don't make cookie cutters in your symbol!)

## DIRECTIONS

### COOKIE CUTTER METHOD

1. Cut your potato in two at the widest point. This will give you the biggest surface to use for your stamp.

2. Press the cookie cutter firmly and deeply into the potato.

3. Carefully cut a thick slice from the potato around the cookie cutter. This thick slice should slide off the potato right up onto the cookie cutter.

4. Carefully remove the cookie cutter from the potato.

5. Leave your potato stamp out for a while to dry, or pat it dry carefully with kitchen paper. Paint won't stick to a wet potato.

## CARVING METHOD

1. Cut your potato in half and pat dry with kitchen paper or leave to air dry until it is touch dry.

2. Draw your pattern onto the potato with a sharp pencil.

3. Carefully start carving. To make this easier, carve the shape of your symbol all the way down the potato as shown in illustration X.

4. For circles, corners, or tricky detailed parts with negative space, take your knife and carve around the edge of the detail with your blade slightly angled in. Carefully dig the point of your knife into the circle and twist to remove the negative parts of the symbol. Gently does it, you don't want to ruin your stamp!

## NOW, ON TO THE STAMPING

5. Place some paper or plastic over the table you're using, especially if you're printing on fabric. No matter what you're stamping on, it can be a messy process, and I guarantee if you're stamping on material that the paint will go through the fabric.

6. There are two ways to ink your stamp. Squeeze out a bit of paint onto a piece of scrap cardboard or plastic and then dip the stamp into it, or using a paint brush or roller, apply paint straight onto your stamp, making sure you wipe away any paint that gathers at the edges. Try out both and see which you prefer—the dipping method can result in a bit more bleed of the paint.

7. Experiment with your new stamp on a scrap of fabric. After a couple of tries, you'll know how hard you need to press your stamp to get the thickness of paint you're looking for.

8. Now stamp your fabric or paper.

9. If you want to change colors, wipe off as much of the original paint as you can using a paper towel before applying a second color.

10. Remember that fabric paint usually needs ironing to set it. Read the instructions on your paint carefully if you haven't used it before.

11. Once your paint is dry, you might like to outline your symbol with a dark marker to really bring out the image.

## TINY PENNANTS!

You can combine your newly earned potato stamping skills with your new pennant making skills (see the pennant project on page 83) to make tiny pennants! Depending on the size of your stamp, you can use bamboo skewers, take-out chopsticks, or found twigs for the pole at the top and embroidery thread for the ribbon.

You can also add a tiny dot of glue to your thread if you're worried about the knot coming undone or sliding up and down the pole.

# CHAPTER EIGHT

# Paste-ups

Paste-ups (also known as Wheat Pastes) are, at their most basic, pieces of paper glued to walls. In a way, they recall the craft techniques of collage (gluing paper cut outs to other paper) and decoupage (gluing paper cutouts to an item of furniture or bric-a-brac). The craft of decoupage can be traced back to the tomb art of East Siberia, where nomadic tribes would cut out felt shapes to decorate the tombs of their deceased, and to twelfth-century China, where paper cutouts were used to decorate boxes, windows, lanterns, and other objects.

Your paste-ups can consist of anything on paper—drawings, collage, printouts of text or photos (although photographic paper doesn't tend to stick very well), or a mixture of all of these. They can be as big or as small as you like, and they can be on plain paper, scrap paper, newspaper, or vintage advertising. You can even try your hand at paste-ups using things like paper doilies, flattened cup-cake paper pans, wrapping paper… Basically, if it's on or made of paper, you can paste it up!

If you're feeling truly inspired, try experimenting with different glues to see what will hold up material like doilies or crochet. Textile paste-ups tend to stick better if you leave the material in the glue for a little while to allow it to soak into the fabric.

Use a potato stamp (page 137) to make a quick and fast repeated image for paste-ups. If you're using pens to draw on your paper, make sure they don't run when wet, otherwise you'll ruin your piece when you try to paste it up.

A quick note about location—brick and stucco walls usually work best—the flatter and smoother the wall surface, the better. Pasting on surfaces like wooden fences won't work very well as the rough wooden surface isn't the best for holding glue and paper. But try stuff out, experiment, and see what works best for you!

RANDOM
ACTS OF
GENTLE
ANARCHY
COMMIT
NO
NUISANCE
Thanks boys,
I've got this one...

These three paste-ups are included at the back of this book in the patterns section on page 204. The top paste-up is a photograph of a guerrilla mosaic I made under the careful eye of UK anarchist ceramist Carrie Reichardt, which was inspired by the words of comedian Bill Hicks. The lower left paste-up is a copy of a government sanctioned sign painted in the alleys of Melbourne during the mid-nineteenth century which can still be found around the city today if you know where to look. Similar signs appeared in London with a reverse color scheme. Although the signs are intended to read "Commit No Nuisance," it has been a common practice of anonymous members of the public to paint out the word "No," leaving the sign to communicate the opposite of its original intent. The first time I came across one of these signs as a teenager down a cobblestone alley, it bade me to Commit Nuisance, which delighted my heart no end.

The lower right paste-up is of a princess who's actively rescuing herself rather than waiting to be rescued and is based on a drawing from a medieval manuscript.

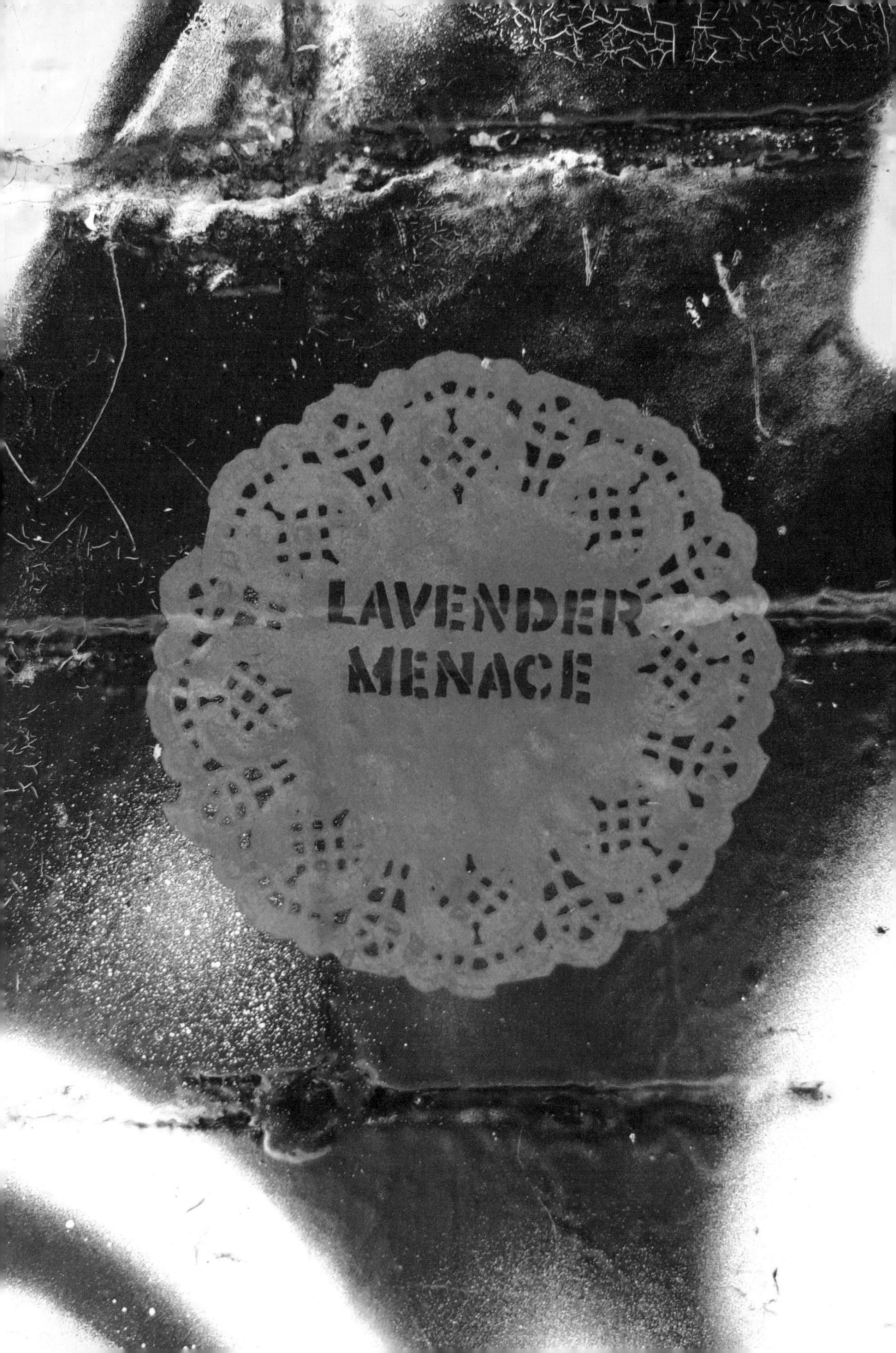
LAVENDER
MENACE

# Paste-ups

## WHAT YOU'LL NEED

*Paper paste-up*

*Carpenters/white/PVA (polyvinyl acetate) glue[1] (it's not expensive, and you can get it from most art/craft/hardware stores)*

*Water*

*Leakproof container with a lid (I like to use a plastic container with a screw top lid; best to use one you don't want to use for food ever again)*

*Paintbrush (the best type to use is a big thick one, like a housepainter's paintbrush; the larger size of the brush makes the application of the glue much faster)*

## DIRECTIONS

1. Mix the glue and water in about a 50/50 ratio in the container. You want it to be fluid and not lumpy. Stir until it's well mixed.

2. Close your container firmly, as it needs to travel to your location without leaking (hopefully!)

3. When positioned at your wall, first paint a patch of glue on the wall itself which is slightly bigger than the size of your piece. Make sure you layer it on it well, now is not the time to be frugal with the glue.

4. Place the piece of paper on the glue patch, and paint another layer of glue over the top. As you do this, smooth out as many wrinkles as you can. Accept, however, there may be some wrinkles you can't get out. The paper will tighten as it dries, which usually gets rid of any smaller wrinkles you couldn't get out in this step anyway.

5. You will probably want to photograph it, this is best done when it's dry. It shouldn't take too long to dry, depending on the weather and where you are. Wait a little and then come back to photograph your activism out in the world. Easy!

A quick aside about stickers. Covering something with stickers is a familiar craft for kids and teenagers, and it's simple to do as activism. When stickers are being used for activism or graffiti, they are sometimes referred to as "slaps" or "slap-ups," named for the speed and style of their installation. You can draw or print your own slaps at home, potato stamp them, or get slaps professionally printed (depending on how many you want). Be sure to experiment with different types of printable homemade stickers to learn which brands survive best when exposed to the weather.

1 People also use a mixture of flour and water or flour, water, and sugar. Unfortunately, slugs and snails find these wheat paste solutions very tasty and will eat your paste-up while munching on the glue. Whatever's left can also go moldy when exposed to weather.

## Lavender Menace

The term "Lavender Menace" was first used in 1969 by the National Organization for Women's president Betty Friedan to describe the threat she believed lesbians posed to NOW and the emerging women's movement. She felt that the stereotype of the "man-hating" lesbian would provide an easy reason to dismiss the seriousness of the organization's political work, and so NOW began distancing itself from lesbian causes. In return, a small group of lesbian feminists embraced the term, wrote a manifesto entitled "The Woman-Identified Woman," and screen printed pale purple T-shirts with the words "Lavender Menace" for the group to wear as they rushed the stage of the Second Congress to Unite Women, a conference which didn't feature a single open lesbian on the bill. They took to the microphone to tell the audience how angry they were about the exclusion of lesbians from the conference and from the women's movement as a whole. They were invited back the next day to run workshops on lesbian rights and homophobia. The Lavender Menace is often identified as a founding moment for lesbian feminism.

#Lavendermenace

# CHAPTER NINE

# Baking

So, you're going to a party or hosting a get-together and you want to raise some issues or stir up trouble? Alternatively, maybe you want to raise a little cash for a favorite cause with a bake sale and you want it themed appropriately.

You might want to make some seditious cupcakes, some activist cookies, or some pies with something to say?

Don't think that this is the only way to combine your activism and your baking, however! These are just three approaches, but there's heaps of other ways to do it too. For example, do a quick internet search for "bread stenciling," and with your newfound stencil knowledge from chapter 7, the pie's the limit!

I'm going to be honest with you, I haven't baked anything since I was a child, so this was all pretty new to me too. But if I can try it and succeed, you can too.

PS: Everything was delicious.

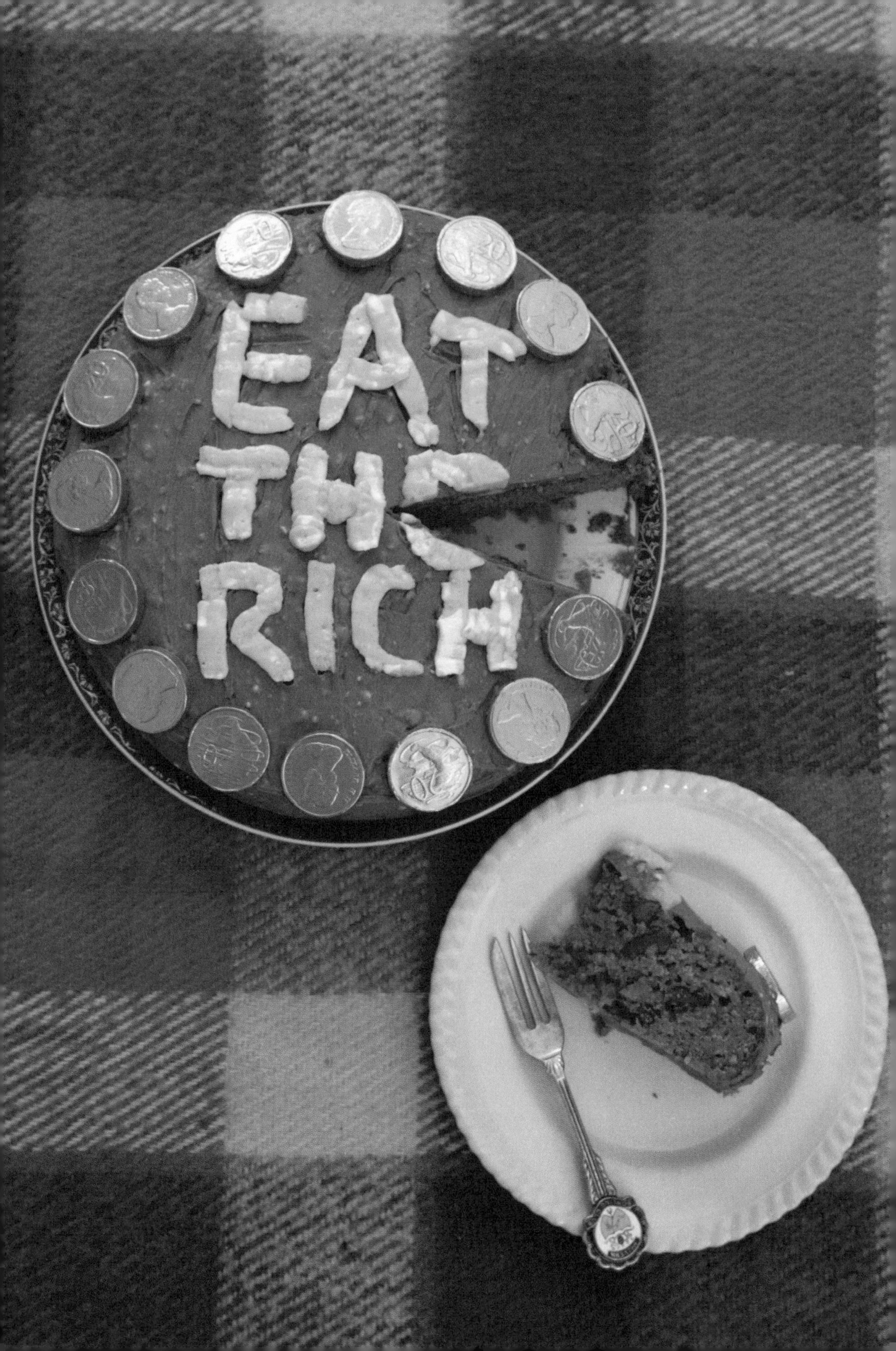
EAT
THE
RICH

# Decorating Cakes

## WHAT YOU'LL NEED

### For the cake

¼ cup raisins

¼ cup of orange juice

3 cups grated carrots

1 cup of brown sugar

1 cup of vegetable oil

3 eggs

2 cups plain flour

1½ tsp. baking powder

½ tsp. baking soda

1 tsp. ground nutmeg

2 tsp. ground cinnamon

¼ cup chopped walnuts

¼ cup chopped pecans

### For the icing

2 cups (500g) cream cheese
at room temperature
1 stick (100g) unsalted
butter at room temperature
½ cup confectioners/icing/
powdered sugar

Food coloring

### For the decorating

Piping bag or
small ziplock bag

### Optional

Candy or
wrapped chocolates

When we were young, we had a cake decorating book from which our mum would let us choose the cake we wanted for our birthday that year. I like that I can keep that tradition alive with an activist bent.

For this slogan, I've chosen a carrot cake (get it? "carat" is the unit of weight for diamonds and gemstones, and "karat" is the unit of purity of gold), but you can use any cake recipe for your activism. You could also make cupcakes, depending on your design, your slogans and your ultimate goal for the cakes.

## DIRECTIONS

### MAKING THE CAKE

1. Preheat your oven to 320 degrees F (160 degrees C).

2. Soak raisins in the orange juice for 20 minutes.

3. Oil and flour an 8-inch (20-centimeter) cake pan.

4. Combine carrot, sugar, oil, and eggs in a bowl.

5. In another bowl, combine flour, baking powder, baking soda, cinnamon, and nutmeg.

6. Add the carrot mixture to the flour mixture and stir.

7. Add the nuts and raisins and mix well.

8. Pour into the pan and cook for 50 mins or until a skewer poked into the middle of the cake comes out clean.

9. Leave to cool in the tin for 10 minutes, then transfer to a cooling rack to completely cool.

## MAKING THE ICING

1. Combine the cream cheese and butter in a mixer and mix on high until well blended. Make sure the ingredients are at room temperature so they will mix together properly. Do as I say, not at I do! The little white spots in the photo are small lumps of cream cheese that didn't combine properly because it was still a little cold.

2. Reduce speed and add sugar, then beat until everything is combined

3. Turn off mixer and divide icing into as many bowls as the number of colors you're using. My design is mostly purple and a bit less than one-third yellow.

4. Add food coloring to each bowl of icing and mix well.

5. Ice cake with your main color.

6. Put second color icing in a piping bag; if you don't have one, a ziplock bag works fine. Put your icing in the bag and squeeze it down to one corner. Snip off a tiny bit of the corner to create a hole to squeeze out the icing.

7. Pipe on your letters. If this is your first time icing, do a test letter or two on a plate first.

8. If required, decorate cake further with candy or wrapped chocolates.

### Eat the Rich

"Eat the rich" was a slogan popular in the late 1960s and early 1970s with anarchists and other activists. It comes from a saying attributed to Enlightenment philosopher Jean-Jacques Rousseau (1712–1778) "When the people shall have nothing more to eat, they will eat the rich."

As with Riots Not Diets, it's not meant to be taken literally.

give peas a chance
I'm vegan Bite me
Powered by PLANTS
Oh KALE NO!
Eat beans Not beings

# Protest Cookies

## WHAT YOU'LL NEED

### For the cake

2 ¼ cups of all-purpose (plain) flour

2 tsp. ground ginger

heaping ½ tsp. ground nutmeg

1 tsp. ground cinnamon

¼ tsp. ground cloves

½ tsp. baking soda

¾ cup of vegetable oil

¼ cup molasses

a few Tbsp. of non-dairy milk

### For the icing

2½ Tbsp. of the liquid from a can of garbanzo beans, aka chick peas (I promise the icing won't taste like beans!)

2 cups confectioners/icing/ powdered sugar

food coloring

### For decorating

cake decorating pens

wooden skewers or clean ice cream sticks

Feel free to use your favorite cookie recipe for this project, but bear in mind that additions like nuts, chocolate, and candy will result in lumpy cookies, which makes decorating them more difficult. A flat cookie makes a better canvas for your message.

I love gingerbread, so here's my favorite recipe. I like them spicy, but if you're not so keen on that, you can halve the quantities of the spices to make the cookies lighter.

The type of icing is important to make your little cookie placards easy to decorate. Royal icing is the most effective, and the royal icing in this recipe is a great vegan substitute. If you're going down the vegan path with these, make sure your coloring and decorations don't have animal products in them too!

Some vegan recipes call for specialty products, but this one's ingredients are all just simple foods you can find in any supermarket. To decorate it, I used a food grade felt tip pen. These can be found in cake decorating stores or online, and the brand I used, AmeriColor, is a vegan product.

VEGAN GINGERBREAD

## DIRECTIONS

### MAKING THE COOKIES

1. Preheat your oven to 350 degrees F (180 degrees C).

2. Line your cookie sheet with baking paper.

3. Place the flour, spices and baking soda into a bowl and mix together.

4. Add in the oil and molasses and stir until mixture comes together.

5. If the mixture is too dry, add one Tbsp. of non-dairy milk at a time until the dough comes together.

6. Flour your board and rolling pin and roll mixture to ¼ inch (½ centimeters) thick.

7. Cut the dough into rectangles 2 inches by 2½ inches
(5 centimeters x 6 centimeters).

8. Place cookies on cookie sheet; bake for 15 minutes.

9. Once you take them out of the oven, leave to cool on the cookie sheet for a few minutes; then with a wooden skewer/ice cream stick, carefully poke a hole into each cookie where the placard handle will be placed later.

10. Transfer to a cooling rack until completely cooled.

## MAKING THE ICING

This vegan royal icing doesn't set quite as hard as the egg version but still works great as a background for your cookie signs.

1. Whisk the garbanzo bean liquid until foamy (about 30 seconds in a mixer, a little longer by hand).

2. Add in the confectioner's sugar; stir slowly until combined.

3. To make the icing thicker, add more sugar. If you want it runnier, add more garbanzo bean liquid.

4. Divide into small bowls, one for each color you're making.

5. Add a drop or two of food coloring and mix well. You can add more drops to make the color darker, but if it's too dark, the pens won't show up against the icing.

## ICING THE COOKIES

1. Using the back (non-serrated) edge of a table knife, ice the cookies.

2. Dip the end of each wooden skewer/ice cream stick into the icing and then push into the hole you made before the cookies were cool.

## DECORATING YOUR COOKIES

Once you've iced your cookies, pop them in the fridge for 20 minutes or so for the icing to firm up. Then decorate with your slogans! If you've used the vegan icing, don't press too hard with the pens, otherwise you might break through the top crust of the icing.

**Veganism**

Vegans don't use any animal products at all. They don't eat meat or other animal products such as dairy, eggs, or honey and don't use products such as leather. Vegans do this for a variety of reasons; some don't believe that animal lives should be taken when there are other substitutes available, others feel that the industrial farming of animals is environmentally damaging and unsustainable. The term itself was coined when in 1944 several members of the British Vegetarian Society (founded in 1843) asked if a section of their newsletter could be devoted to non-dairy vegetarianism. The request was denied, so Donald Watson, secretary of the Leicester branch, set up his own newsletter called *The Vegan News*, "vegan" being a word he had made up himself.

Visit this site to get started: http://vegankit.com/.

World Vegan Day is celebrated November 1. Learn more by visiting: http://wvd.org.au/.

#vegan #veganfood #whatfatveganseat

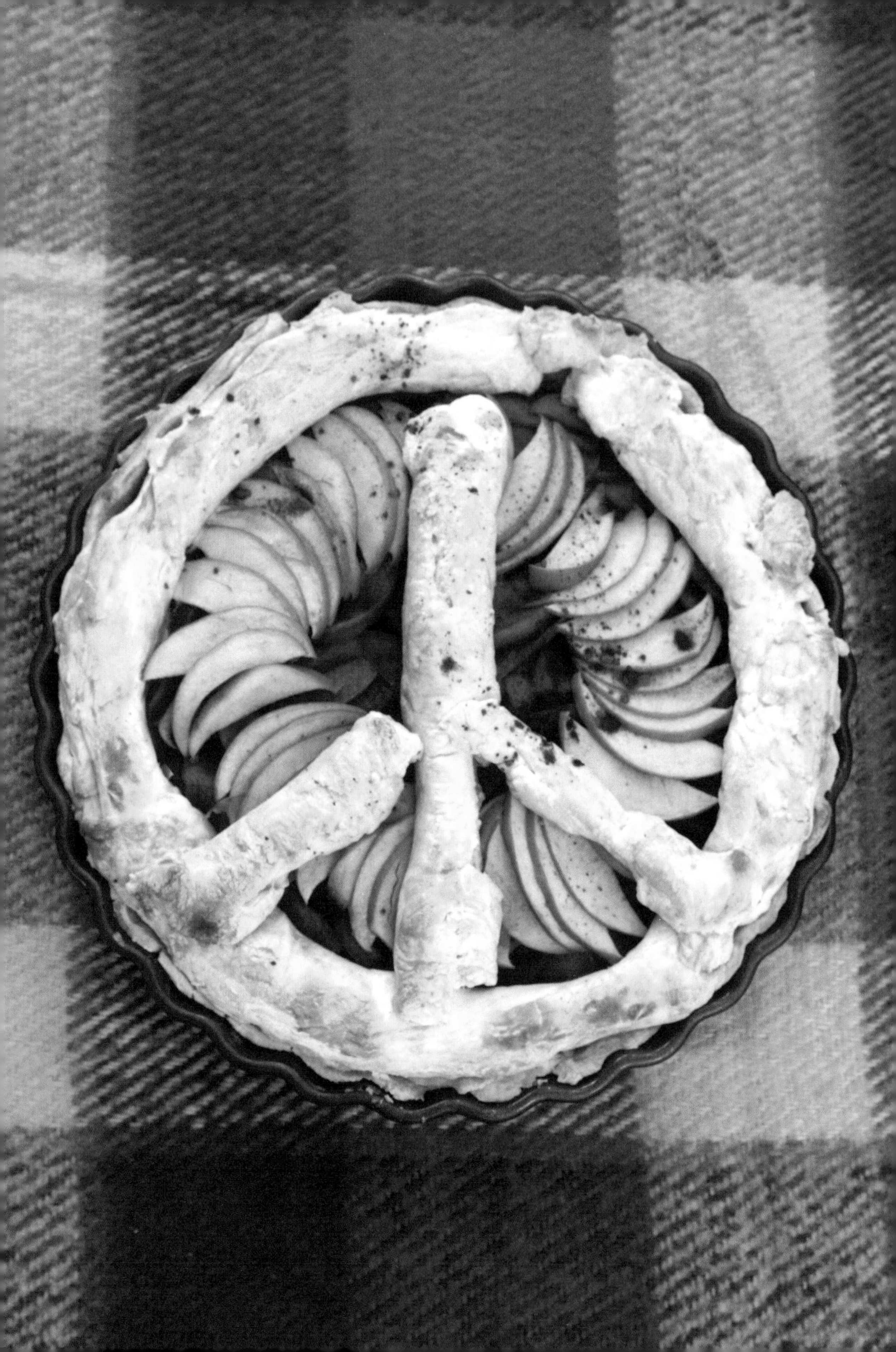

# Pie Tops

## WHAT YOU'LL NEED

*Pie pan approximately 10 inches (25 centimeters)*

*Pastry
(I used 2 sheets of frozen pastry bought from a store, but make your own if you're up for it!)*

*Approx. 1½ cups dried beans or rice for blind baking*

*2–3 apples
(depending on the size and depth of your pie pan)*

*1 cup dark brown sugar (you can also use brown/ raw sugar)*

*1½ cups of water*

*¼ tsp. of vanilla paste or extract*

*Parchment paper for baking*

*1 egg (or alternatively oil, milk, non-dairy milk, melted butter, or margarine) for the egg wash*

*Pastry brush*

*Ground cinnamon*

This works with any type of pie, and you can make them small or large. I've chosen an apple pie, but feel free to substitute your favorite pie instead. Here, I've used a single symbol for my pie, but you could also cover the pie with a layer of pastry and cut letters and words out to place on top in addition to or instead of a symbol.

## DIRECTIONS

1. Preheat oven to 350 degrees F (180 degrees C).

2. Grease and flour your pie pan.

3. Cut out pastry and line your pie pan with it. Use a fork to prick your pastry all over, and then place a piece of parchment paper into the pan.

4. Fill pan with dried beans and bake for 10 mins, then carefully remove beans and paper. Bake for an additional 5–10 minutes until pastry is done (it'll look golden).

5. While the pastry is in the oven, thinly slice the apples.

6. Simmer water and sugar together until the sugar has dissolved.

7. Add apples and vanilla; simmer until apples are soft (around 5 minutes or so should do it).

8. When the pastry is done baking, use a slotted spoon to take the apple slices out of the cooking liquid and place them in the pie. Don't throw out the cooking liquid, it makes a lovely syrup when serving the pie.

9. Cut pastry shapes out and place on top of the pie. (Here I also sliced up another apple and laid in it a circle design under the peace sign to give the pie another visual element.)

10. Whisk an egg (or your preferred "egg" wash substitute) and brush onto pastry with the pastry brush. This helps brown the pastry and makes the pie look tasty.

11. Sprinkle cinnamon across the top of the pie. A pinch sifted between your fingers will work better than tipping it out of the jar. (Can you guess which one I tried?)

12. Place pie back in the oven for a further 20–30 minutes until the new pastry is cooked.

13. Serve with sides and toppings to taste.

**Peace Sign**

This peace sign was first designed by British artist Gerald Holtom in 1958 for the Campaign for Nuclear Disarmament. The symbol was based on two letters, "N" and "D" from semaphore, which was a naval alphabet system based on a person signaling with two hand held flags held in particular patterns. The letters stand for Nuclear Disarmament.

# CHAPTER TEN

# Badges, Pins, and Brooches

They're called different things in different countries, but whatever you call them, a badge can be a small but firm statement in support of your cause. There are, of course, dozens of different ways to make them, I'm just starting you off with two. Grab some supplies and create some of these tiny personal statements that you can wear every day.

THEY/THEM

# Felt Badges and Pins

## WHAT YOU'LL NEED

*Pattern (page 232)*
*Colored felt for the bubble*
*Darker felt for the backing*
*Needle and thread*
*Embroidery thread*
*Scissors*
*Pins*
*Safety pin or brooch back*

Felt is one of the easiest materials to work with. It's fairly cheap, you don't need to hem it because it doesn't fray, and it comes in a myriad of bright colors. It can be used by itself or in conjunction with embroidery, sequins, or beads to make badges and pins and add an extra dimension to your activism. Once made, they can be stitched right onto clothing, bags, hats, or any other fabric, or you can add a safety pin or brooch back to make your buttons and badges easily transferable from one jacket to the next!

## DIRECTIONS

1. Photocopy and cut out the speech bubble paper pattern found on page 232. You can point the tail of the speech bubble to whatever direction you need by flipping the paper pattern over or spinning it around. So versatile!

2. Pin your pattern to the felt and cut out.

3. Pin your pattern to the backing felt and cut out.

4. Backstitch your letters. When stitching your words, you can either freehand stitch them onto the felt or sketch them out on the paper pattern first to plan it out.

5. (Optional) You can decorate the speech bubble with sequins or beads as well.

6. Position the backing felt against the back of the speech bubble and pin together.

7. Stitch the two pieces of felt together—you can use a contrasting or matching color thread.

The easiest way to do this is to sew a safety pin to the back of the fabric. Make sure you don't stitch all the way through the badge—you don't want the backing stitches to show through the front design.

Remember to make sure you're sewing the correct arm of the safety pin to the back of the badge. I find it helps to open the pin first and check. This may sound obvious, but I've managed to stitch the wrong side on a number of occasions, so I do this check each time.

There are also special brooch backs you can buy at craft stores if you prefer that to a safety pin. They are attached to the brooch the same way.

## Pronouns

A person's pronouns are just as important to get right as their name. Using the wrong pronoun can misgender a person, which can make them feel that their identity is being invalidated and/or that they are being disrespected or dismissed. There are dozens of different pronouns, and it's not always apparent which pronoun a person prefers. A private and polite enquiry is a sure way to get someone's pronouns correct, or simply using gender-neutral "they/them" pronouns is often acceptable.

## Pink Triangle

The pink triangle pointing downward was originally used in Nazi concentration camps as a badge to identify male prisoners who were sent to the camps because of their homosexuality. However, in the late 1970s, the pink triangle was reclaimed as a symbol of pride and began to be used in gay rights protests. Modern use of the symbol has strengthened the original light pink color to hot pink, and it is sometimes inverted so the triangle points upwards.

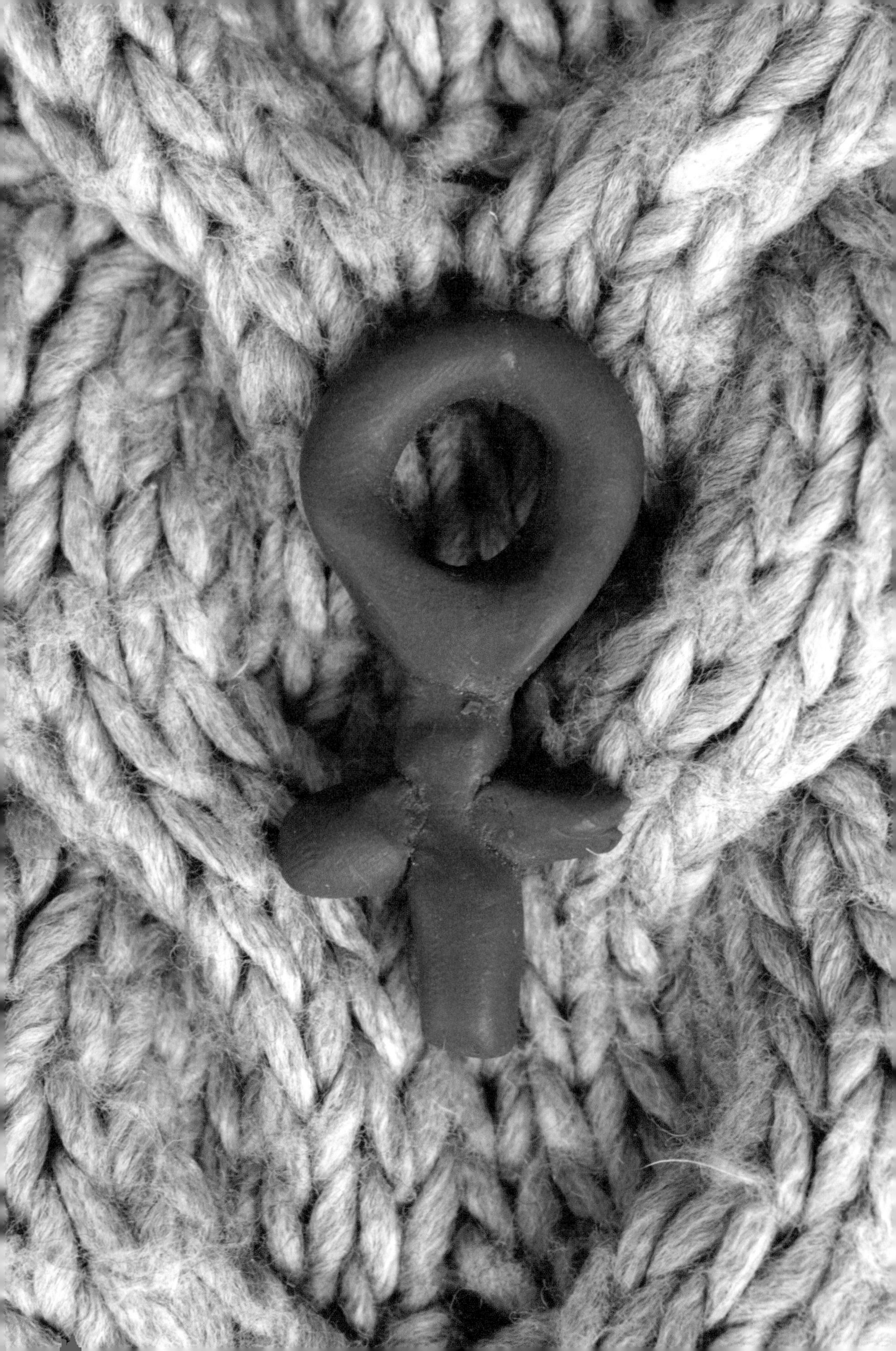

# Polymer Clay Brooches

## WHAT YOU'LL NEED

*Polymer clay*

*Brooch back*

*Two-part epoxy resin glue*

*Scrap piece of cardboard*

*Aluminum foil or parchment paper for baking*

*Mixing stick*

### Optional

*Scrap paper and pencil for designing*

*Wooden skewer*

If you're looking for a more solid style brooch, then polymer clay is a great medium. The polymer comes as a (fairly) soft and malleable product in a wide range of colors, and it is baked hard in a kitchen oven. The baking time and temperatures depend on the brand, so make sure you read the instructions when your creation is ready to bake! To attach your brooch back, all you need is a two-part epoxy resin glue. If you're not familiar with glues, this can sound a little daunting, but it's just a glue that comes in two tubes, and then you mix it together on a piece of scrap cardboard with a stick, toothpick, or wooden skewer to activate the chemicals. Then it's ready to apply to the brooch back to glue it to the brooch. These glues can be found at hardware stores and most supermarkets.

## DIRECTIONS

1. Decide on your design. If this is your first go with polymer clay, pick something simple. You can plan it out on paper or just wing it.

2. The polymer clay can sometimes be quite firm when you start, so roll it around in your hands for a bit to warm it up.

3. Start shaping your brooch. For the women's symbol, I started with a long thin snake. For the Pussy Riot mask, I made a little sphere and then flattened it with my thumb. To make the pattern on the mask and to create the holes, I used the pointy end of a wooden skewer.

4. While you're shaping your brooch, make sure that there is somewhere at the back of the brooch that is long and flat enough to position your brooch back when the time comes. Also, the thicker the clay shape, the longer it will take to bake and the heavier it will be to wear. I try to make them no thicker than 3/8 inches (1 centimeter).

5. If you want to join different bits of the clay together, there are several methods, but the easiest is to just press them together. In the heat of the oven, the clay will fuse together. If you prefer, once you're finished shaping your brooch, you can let it sit overnight before baking to help with the bond.

6. Line your baking tray with aluminum foil or parchment paper to protect your baking sheet from the clay. If you're planning to make a lot of polymer clay pieces, consider buying a baking sheet from a secondhand store specifically for the clay.

7. Bake as per packet instructions.

8. Allow to cool thoroughly (again, how long this takes will depend on the thickness of your brooch).

9. Mix up your two-part epoxy resin as per packet instructions.

10. Apply the resin to the brooch back and glue to it the back of the brooch.

11. Wait for the resin to dry.

12. Wear it proudly, give it as a gift, or leave it somewhere as an act of guerrilla kindness.

# CHAPTER ELEVEN

# Making for Good

There are lots of ways to put your crafting skills to good use for those in need. You can do this on your own: organize a "Making for Good" party with crafty friends or neighbors, get your online community making together, or even coordinate a drop-in crafting workshop at your local community center or church. There are always lots of places that would love to benefit from your crafting skills and enthusiasm (although remember to check with them before you start—you don't want all your hard work to go to waste!).

For example, often a local animal shelter will need blankets for their animals to sleep on. Some shelters send animals to their new home with the blanket they've been using to give them something familiar and comfortable while they're getting used to their new home. If you have a local women's refuge or asylum seeker center, they also sometimes need blankets or toys. Furthermore, you could run a stall at your local markets; sell items you've made and donate the proceeds to your favorite charity.

Ask who is around you that might need your craft. For instance, in Melbourne, we have a huge number of charity drives that crafters can contribute to. Three of my favorites are:

The annual toy drive Softies for Mirabel organized by the Mirabel foundation. Mirabel is a charity that addresses the needs of children who have been orphaned or abandoned as a result of parental drug use. Softies for Mirabel, created by crafter and author Pip Lincoln, is an annual toy drive for anyone who wants to knit, crochet, or sew a softie to be given to Mirabel children.

Learn more at: www.mirabelfoundation.org.au/events-campaigns/softies-for-mirabel.

St. Kilda Mums is a charity that supports children and parents in need. They accept donations including baby clothes, toys, prams, and cots. They encourage the reuse of baby and children's gear to share the joy of parenting and also to help conserve resources. St. Kilda Mums accepts handmade items such as cot blankets and linen, baby wraps, clothing sizes 0–12, and even hand-knitted or crocheted squares that they can stitch into blankets.

Learn more at: www.stkildamums.org.

The lovely Handmade for Humans market is where crafters, artists, and other makers-of-things come together to support asylum seekers in Australia. Every couple of months, Handmade for Humans puts a call out for beautiful handmade goods and treasures that they sell to raise money for RISE (Refugees, Survivors and Ex-detainees). RISE is the first refugee and asylum seeker organization to be run and governed by refugees, asylum seekers, and ex-detainees.

Learn more at: www.facebook.com/creatingawelcome & www.riserefugee.org

A note about communities in times of disaster. When something catastrophic has just happened to a community, you might feel the need to help by reaching for the knitting needles or your sewing machine. It's important to note, however, that just after a disaster, people might need specific things first, especially shelter, food, warm clothes, or medical attention. When a disaster first strikes, it's important to get out of the way of the emergency services and volunteers who are on the ground. Take a moment to think about what the victims of the disaster or the first responders actually need to cope with their immediate situation. If you are able to, volunteer your time to help or send money to the charities and organizations working directly with the communities involved. There's always time for activism afterwards. Don't let your need to do something eclipse the needs of those affected by tragedy.

So, who around you could do with a little handmade support or a donation raised by crafty means?

# CHAPTER TWELVE

# Barter

Not all activism has to be broadcast and not everything you do has to be a public statement. Craftivism can happen in the home and can happen just between two people. One of the things you can use your craft skills for is bartering. Barter, like guerrilla kindness, is a radical decommodification of social relationships and momentarily reclaims the humanity of our actions. Transactions and agreements don't have to be subject to market forces. Instead they can remain tiny, private agreements between two people.

For example, I bartered this hand sewn, paper pieced, 3 foot (1 meter) wide quilt for tattoos from my excellent tattooist Lara. I often take my friend and hairdresser Elinor homemade sweet chili jam or preserves in exchange for doing my hair. Elinor does awesome work from home and is happy to accept tasty treats or crafty items in exchange for her skills. The embroidered witch doily on page 75 was a trade with my friend Sab for looking after our dog one weekend.

And while I buy some of the fabric, ingredients, and items needed to make what I'm bartering with, some also come from my house or fabric stash (or other trades I've done in the past). Ultimately, it's the value of the time involved and your skills, not just the items, that you're bartering.

So next time you need something, have a look around your friends and community. Ask yourself what skills they might be interested in sharing with you and what you can offer them in return.

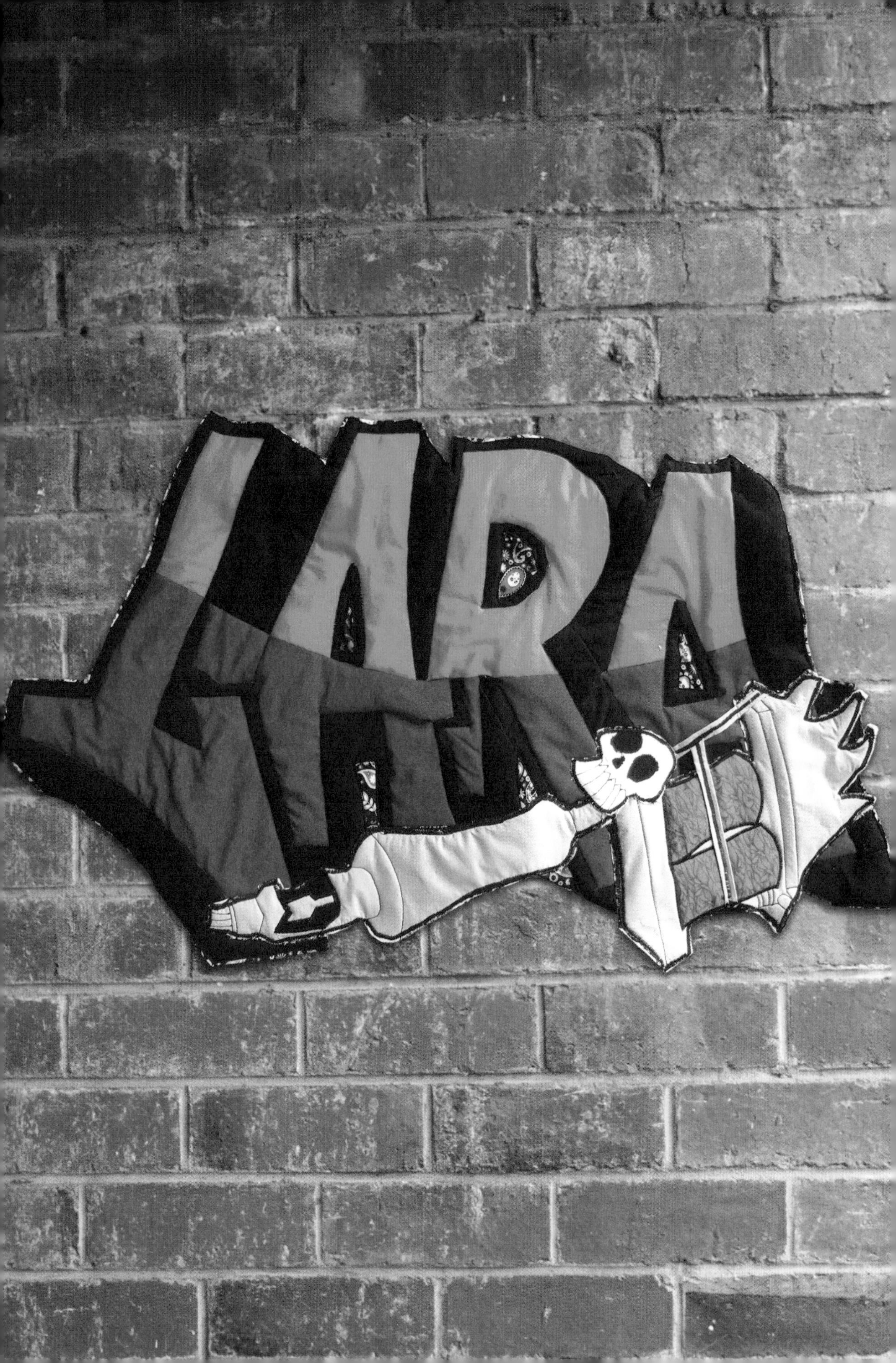

# Afterword

The projects in this book are offered as ideas to get you started expressing your activism craftily. I like to think of them as seeds waiting for you to grow them however you like. Don't think of anything I've suggested as set in stone, rather take these ideas and make them your own. Change the causes and the colors, change the shape and the size, change the placement and the message.

Go out there and change the world with your creative resistance!

**Let me know about your project**

If you upload images of your project to any kind of social media and you'd like me to know about it, tag me in the comments! I'd love to see what you're creating and what you're passionate about. Use the hashtag #CreativeResistanceBook or tag me @sayraphim so I can see the awesome things you're making!

# Acknowledgments

## Acknowledgment of Country

I acknowledge that I was born, live, and work on what always was and always will be the land of the Wurundjeri people of the Kulin nations and that Indigenous sovereignty has never been ceded in Australia. I pay my respects to Elders past, present, and emerging, and I extend that respect to other Aboriginal and Torres Strait Islander peoples as well as to all First Nations people all over the world.

## My massive thanks go out to:

My amazing and super supportive husband, Rob.

My editor Brenda from Mango Publishing, who reached out and offered me the chance of a lifetime.

The super talented Angela East (@jellibat) for her illustrative illustrations.

Betsy Greer, for her tireless efforts celebrating craftivism in all its forms, for inviting me to be in her first ever book on craftivism, and for generously writing a foreword for this book.

Jax Jackie Brown, passionate and amazing queer disability activist and my sensitivity editor for the issues in this book. Also thank you to Anna Branford, who read over the Making for Good chapter, and Astrotwitch and Marshall, who checked over the trans issues.

My talented coven of proofreaders: knitting maestro Caron Wasserfall, crochet and recipe expert Bec Dove, cross stitch radical Rayna Fahey, stitching queen Katti Williams, and especially editor and proofreader extraordinaire Anne-Marie Peard.

Betsy and Bianca for letting me include their beautiful projects in this book.

The awesome Dan Goronszy, who texted me out of the blue and offered to help even though she didn't know what I was working on (thanks for sewing the Suit of Hearts quilt, Dan!)

My amazing circle of friends, who didn't mind random questions via social media about their chosen crafts/passions without any explanation as to why (since the book was still secret at the time), including Marshall Hoxley from Spectrum Cakes, the king of baking; Teegs Rose, the international queen of screen printing; Marina Lychenco, my Russian translator; Erica McCalman and Amy Speirs, for their advice about protocol surrounding the Acknowledgement of Country; my North American terms interpreters, including

Betsy Greer, Leanne Moore, Kim Piper Werker, and especially Jess New and Jess Kilby; and the wonderful Mary Hamilton for being my international cheerleader of amazingness.

The lovely Alison Croggon for all her advice to a new author, and for being someone who didn't mind answering a big pile of questions.

Also to everyone who suggested books for the Activist Library section, especially Julia Feliz, Jessica Walton, Jax Jackie Brown, and Jordi Kerr.

And to my friend and boss Dave Lamb, who has always been so supportive and encouraging about my work and who was super understanding when I needed to swap shifts or take time off to write the book and make the projects.

To the very generous Tiara Paedia, Ming-Zhu Hii, and Alex Loki for discussing one of my ideas for this book and helping me decide on a better path, and to the crafty Beka Hannah who suggested the perfect alternative.

And the super lovely street artist Barek for teaching me paste-ups a couple of years ago during an artist residency.

Also to Kelli from Carbone Master Tailors for all the suit swatches and for being just as enthusiastic about Wagga quilts as I am.

Also to Julia Feliz for amplifying the conversation about privilege that the craftivism movement really needed to have.

To all the activists around the world who fight every single day for a myriad of causes in a myriad of ways, and to my mum Cristine, who sparked the fires of activism in my heart from a very early age.

And to you, most excellent reader, for picking up this book, for wanting to help change the world and for reading all the way to the end of this page.

# Activism Library

## Craftivism and creative activism

Brass, Elaine and Poklewski Koziell, Sophie, *Gathering Force: DIY Culture, Radical Action for Those Tired of Waiting*, The Big Issue, 1997.

Corbett, Sarah, *A Little Book of Craftivism*, Cicada Books, 2013.

Fahey, Rayna, *Really Cross Stitch: For when you just want to stab something a lot*, Herbert Press, 2017.

Flood, Catherine and Grindon, Gavin, *Disobedient Objects*, V & A Publishing, 2014.

Greer, Betsy (ed.), *Craftivism: The Art and Craft of Activism*, Arsenal Pulp Press, 2014.

Hamilton, Clive, *What Do We Want? The Story of Protest in Australia*, National Library of Australia, 2016.

McIntyre, Iain, *How To Make Trouble and Influence People: Pranks, Protests, Graffiti & Political Mischief Making from across Australia*, PM Press, 2009.

Piper Werker, Kim, *Make It Mighty Ugly: Exercises and Advice for Getting Creative Even When It Ain't Pretty*, Sasquatch Books, 2014.

Portwood-Stacer, Laura, *Lifestyle Politics and Radical Activism*, Continuum Publishing Corporation, 2013.

Prain, Leanne and Moore, Mandy, *Yarn Bombing: The Art of Crochet and Knit Graffiti*, Arsenal Pulp Press, 2009.

Sørensen, Majken, *Humour in Political Activism: Creative Nonviolent Resistance*, Palgrave Macmillan, 2016.

Tapper, Joan, *Craft Activism, people, ideas and projects from the new community of handmade and how you can join in*, Potter Craft, 2011.

Wilson, Katherine, *Tinkering: Australians Reinvent DIY Culture*, Monash University Publishing, 2017.

## For young activists

Brown, Lyn Mikel, *Powered by Girl: A Field Guide for Supporting Youth Activists*, Beacon Press, 2016.

Favilli, Elena and Cavallo, Francesca, *Good Night Stories for Rebel Girls (Volume 1 and 2)*, Timbuktu Labs, 2016.

Huegal, Kelly, *GLBTQ: The Survival Guide for Gay, Lesbian, Bisexual, Transgender, and Questioning Teens*, Free Spirit Publishing, 2011.

McBride Johnson, Harriet, *Accidents of Nature*, Henry Holt and Co., 2006.

Nagara, Innosanto, *A is for Activist*, Seven Stories Press, 2013.

Newman, Lesléa, *Daddy, Papa and Me*, Tricycle Press, 2008.

Newman, Lesléa, *Mommy, Mama and Me*, Tricycle Press, 2009.

Pessin-Whedbee, Brook, *Who Are You? The Kid's Guide to Gender Identity*, Jessica Kingsley Publishers, 2016.

Savage, Sarah, *Are you a girl or a boy?*, Jessica Kingsley Publishers, 2017.

Walton, Jess, and MacPherson, Dougal, *Introducing Teddy: A Gentle Story About Gender and Friendship* Bloomsbury USA Children's, 2016.

## Guerrilla Kindness chapter

Jocelyn, Marthe, *Sneaky Art, Crafty surprises to hide in plain sight*, Candlewick Press, 2013.

Smith, Keri, *The Guerrilla Art Kit*, Princeton Architectural Press, 2007.

Wallace, Danny, *Join Me: The True Story of a Man Who Started a Cult by Accident*, Ebury Publishing, 2003.

## Knitting and Crochet chapter

Cooper, Charlotte, *Fat Activism: A Radical Social Movement*, Hammer/On Press, 2016.

Greer, Betsy, *Knitting for Good*, Trumpeter, 2008.

Gessen, Masha, *Words Will Break Cement, the passion of Pussy Riot*, Granta Publications, 2014.

Macdonald, Anne L., *No Idle Hands, the social history of American knitting*, Ballantine Books, 1988.

Rothblum, Esther and Solovay, Sondra (eds.), *The Fat Studies Reader*, NYU Press, 2009.

Deadly Knitshade, *Knit The City: A Whodunnknit Set in London*, Summersdale, 2011.

## Cross stitch and embroidery chapter

Bernstein Sycamore, Mattilda, *Nobody Passes: Rejecting the Rules of Gender and Conformity*, Seal Press, 2006.

Bornstein, Kate, *My New Gender Workbook: A Step-By-Step Guide to Achieving World Peace Through Gender Anarchy and Sex Positivity*, Routledge, 2013.

Bornstein, Kate, and Bergman, S. Bear, *Gender Outlaws: The Next Generation*, Seal Press, 2010.

Eddo-Lodge, Reni, *Why I'm No Longer Talking to White People About Race*, Bloomsbury Circus, 2017.

Grant, Stan, *Talking To My Country*, HarperCollins AU, 2016.

King, Nia and Glennon-Zukoff, Jessica, *Queer and Trans Artists of Colour: Stories of Some of Our Lives*, CreateSpace Independent Publishing Platform, volume 1: 2014, volume 2: 2016.

Land, Claire, *Decolonising Solidarity: Dilemmas and Directions for Supporters of Indigenous Struggles*, Zed Books, 2015.

Lowery, Wesley, *They Can't Kill Us All: The Story of Black Lives Matter*, Penguin Books, 2017.

Moreton-Robinson, Aileen, *Talkin' Up To The White Woman: Indigenous Women And Feminism*, University of Queensland Press, 2002.

Parker, Rozsika, *The Subversive Stitch, embroidery and the making of the feminine*, I. B. Tauris, 1984.

Spade, Dean, *Normal Life: Administrative Violence, Critical Trans Politics, and the Limits of the Law*, Duke University Press Books, 2015.

## Sewing chapter

Boyd, Andrew and Mitchell, Dave Oswald, *Beautiful Trouble: A Toolbox for Revolution*, OR Books, 2016.

Caro, Jane, (ed.), *Destroying the Joint: Why Women Have To Change The World*, ReadHowYouWant, 2014.

Hoffman, Abbie, *Steal This Book*, Pirate Editions/Grove Press, 1971.

McBride Johnson, Harriet, *Too Late To Die Young: Nearly True Tales From A Life*, Picador, 2006.

Syjuco, Stephanie, *Making Fabric Protest Banners, tips + tricks* https://drive.google.com/file/d/0B6g_dTRVOZg6MjhublBhMHh6MFU/view.

## Quilting chapter

Gero, Annette and Somerville, Katie, *The Making of the Australian Quilt, 1800–1950*, National Gallery of Victoria, 2016.

Finley, Ruth E., *Old Patchwork Quilts and the women who made them*, Charles T. Brandford Company, 1929.

Mazloomi, Carolyn L., *And Still We Rise: Race, Culture and Visual Conversations*, Schiffer Publishing Ltd., 2015.

MacDowell, Marsha, Donaldson, Beth, Worral, Mary, and Swanson, Lynne, *Quilts and Human Rights*, University of Nebraska Press, 2016.

## Visible mending chapter

Press, Clare, *Wardrobe Crisis, how we went from Sunday best to fast fashion*, Nero, 2016.

Roach, Kristin M., *Mend It Better: Creative Patching, Darning and Stitching*, Storey Publishing, 2012.

Ministry of Information, *Make Do and Mend (Historic Booklet)*, Sabrestorm Publishing, 2007.

## Stamps and stencils

Ahmed, Sara, *Living a Feminist Life*, Duke University Press, 2017.

Clare, Eli, *Brilliant Imperfection: Grappling with Cure*, Duke University Press, 2017.

McRuer, Robert, *Crip Theory: Cultural Signs of Queerness and Disability*, NYU Press, 2006.

Morris, Jenny, *Pride against Prejudice: A Personal Politics of Disability*, Womens Press Ltd (UK), 1999.

## Baking chapter

Feliz Brueck, Julia, *Veganism in an Oppressive World: A Vegans-of-Colour Community Project*, Sanctuary Publishers, 2017.

Vodeb, Oliver, *Food Democracy: Critical Lessons in Food, Communication, Design and Art*, The University of Chicago Press, 2017.

Taylor, Sunaura, *Beasts of Burden: Animal and Disability Liberation*, The New Press, 2017.

## Badges and pins chapter

Andreyko, Marc, Gaydos, Sarah, Rich, Jamie S. (eds.), *Love is Love,* IDW Publishing, 2017.

Beard, Mary, *Women and Power: A Manifesto,* Profile Books, 2017.

Conrad, Ryan (ed.), *Against Equality: Don't Ask to Fight Their Wars,* Against Equality Press, 2011.

Conrad, Ryan (ed.), *Against Equality: Queer Critics of Gay Marriage,* Against Equality Press, 2010.

Conrad, Ryan (ed.), *Against Equality: Queer Revolution, Not Mere Inclusion,* Against Equality Press, 2014.

Prager, Sarah, *Queer, There and Everywhere: 23 People Who Changed the World,* HarperCollins, 2017.

# Clipping Corners and Curves

Clipping corners helps remove excess bulk of fabric, helps curves lie smoothly and not wrinkle up, and helps makes the item lie flat. When cutting the fabric, cut close to the stitching, but be careful not to cut through the stitches.

## CLIPPING CORNERS

+ **Outer corners:** snip off the corner diagonally.

+ **Inner corners:** cut diagonally into the corner.

## CLIPPING CURVES

There's an old saying to help you remember which cut to do on which curves: "clip valleys, notch mountains."

+ **Convex curves (mountains):** clip notches in a triangle pattern.

+ **Concave curves (valleys):** notch by cutting into the curve.

# How to Knit

**CAST ON**

**Step 1:** To make a slip knot, place yarn as shown (like a pretzel), with the tail of the yarn at the right and the ball of yarn at the left. Insert needle to pick up yarn and draw it through the knot.

**Step 2:** Tug gently on tail end of yarn until it's snug on the left needle. (Left handed people will need to reverse these instructions.)

**Step 3:** Insert right needle through first stitch.

**Step 4:** Wrap yarn around right needle.

**Step 5:** Draw yarn back through first stitch.

**Step 6:** Slide new stitch from right needle back onto left needle.

**Step 7:** Tug gently to ensure stitch is tight. Repeat step 3–7 until you have the correct amount of stitches.

**KNIT**

**Step 1:** Insert right needle through the back of the first stitch.

**Step 2:** Wrap yarn around right needle.

**Step 3:** Draw yarn back through first stitch.

**Step 4:** Keeping the new stitch on right hand needle, slide the old stitch off the left hand needle. Repeat for the rest of the row unless otherwise instructed by the pattern.

PURL

**Step 1:** Insert right needle through the front of the first stitch.

**Step 2:** Wrap yarn around right needle.

**Step 3:** Draw yarn back through first stitch.

**Step 4:** Keeping the new stitch on right hand needle, slide the old stitch off the left hand needle. Repeat for the rest of the row unless otherwise instructed by the pattern.

## SINGLE INCREASE

**Step 1:** Insert needle through stitch and wrap yarn around as usual.

**Step 2:** Draw needle back through the knitting with stitch, but don't slide the stitch off.

**Step 3:** Slide new stitch from right needle back onto left needle.

**Step 4:** New stitch is ready to knit.

## DECREASE

**Step 1:** Insert the needle through the next two stitches and wrap yarn around needle.

**Step 2:** Draw needle back through the knitting to create new stitch on the right hand needle.

**Step 3:** Slide both old stitches off the left hand needle to finish your decrease.

## CHANGING COLORS (FAIR ISLE OR STRANDED TECHNIQUE)

Changing colors in a row is actually much easier than it may look. It works the same for either knitting or purling. The following illustrations are the purl side so you can see what's going on.

When working with a main and a secondary color yarn, it's best to cut an arm's length of your secondary color and use this to avoid balls of yarn getting tangled as you knit.

**Step 1:** Knit row as per usual until you get to the stitch before the secondary color stitch. Insert needle and wrap secondary color yarn around needle.

**Step 2:** Draw yarn back through first stitch and slide the old stitch off the left hand needle.

## SINGLE STITCH IN SECONDARY COLOR

**Step 3:** Bring the primary color yarn along the back of the knitting to knit the next stitch. Be sure not to pull too tightly, otherwise you'll warp the knitting. Continue knitting with the primary color. Once you've reached the end of the row, weave secondary color ends into the back of the knitting.

## SEVERAL STITCHES IN SECONDARY COLOR

**Step 3:** Continue knitting required amount of stitches in secondary color. Then revert to primary color. Ensure all ends are long enough so that you can tie them together to keep the stitches from unravelling.

## TWO COLORS SIDE BY SIDE

When you're knitting two colors side by side for several rows (for instance, the hair beside the face on the Knitted Protest Doll on page 44), there's a special twist you can do with both yarns to stop holes appearing between colors. Again, the illustrations are as seen from the purl side to show you what's going on.

**Step 1:** Knit the row up to the color change. Insert the needle into the new color stitch and pull the yarn of the old color across the new color block.

**Step 2:** Take the new color yarn up from underneath and across the old yarn (there's your twist), and continue to knit the new color.

## CASTING OFF

**Step 1:** From the start of the row, knit two stitches.

**Step 2:** Insert left hand needle into the first stitch and pull that stitch over the second stitch and off the needle.

**Step 3:** Knit next stitch, then repeat step 2 until end of row.

**Step 4:** Snip tail of yarn and pull through final stitch.

# How to Crochet

**Step 1:** To make a slip knot, place yarn as shown (like a pretzel), with the tail of the yarn at the right and the ball of yarn at the left. Insert needle to pick up yarn and draw it through the knot.

**Step 2:** Tug gently on tail end of yarn until it's snug on the crochet hook.

**Step 3:** Wrap yarn around hook once as shown, and pull yarn through loop to create another loop. You now have a single chain stitch. Repeat step 3 until you have crocheted to desired length.

**Step 4:** To join your chain into a circle, simple pass your crochet hook into the first chain, wrap yarn around hook once and pull back through.

**Step 5:** Insert hook through the middle of the circle. Wrap yarn once around hook as shown and pull back through.

**Step 6:** Chain twice more, then for a double (treble in UK/AU), wrap yarn once around hook and insert hook through the middle of the circle.

**Step 7:** Wrap yarn once more around hook and pull back through two loops, leaving two loops on the hook (including the one you just made).

**Step 8:** Wrap yarn once more around hook and pull back through all loops, leaving the loop you just made on the hook.

**Step 9:** Wrap yarn once more around hook and pull back through final loop, leaving the loop you just made on the hook. Repeat double and chain stitches as per pattern.

## CROCHETING DOUBLE (TREBLE IN UK/AU) FOR BUNTING LETTERS

**Step 1:** Once your chain is long enough as per the pattern, wrap yarn around hook once and insert hook into 3rd chain away from hook. You'll end up with three loops on your hook.

**Step 2:** Wrap yarn once around hook and pull through the first loop, leaving three loops on hook (including the one you just made).

**Step 3:** Wrap yarn once more around hook and pull through two loops, leaving two loops on the hook (including the one you just made)

**Step 4:** Finally, wrap yarn one last time around hook and pull through remaining two loops, leaving one loop on the hook (the last one you just made). Insert hook into chain next to the one you were just working from and repeat steps 2–4.

# How to Cross Stitch

Your next needle placement is always marked with an "x."

**Step 1:** Bring your needle up through the fabric from underneath at point A.

**Step 2:** Pass your needle back down through the fabric diagonally across at point B.

**Step 3:** Bring your needle up through the fabric from underneath at point C.

**Step 4:** Pass your needle back down through the fabric diagonally across at point D.

**Step 5:** Tug gently to ensure that the stitch lies flat on the fabric but doesn't pucker it.

**Step 6:** Repeat steps 1–4.

# How to Back Stitch

Your next needle placement is always marked with an "x."

**Step 1:** Bring your needle up through the fabric from behind/ underneath.

**Step 2:** Pass the needle back down through the fabric about ¼ inch (½ centimeter) from the start. This is your first stitch.

**Step 3:** Bring your needle through the fabric from underneath about ¼ inch (½ centimeter) away from your first stitch.

**Step 4:** Pass your needle back down through the fabric just next to the end of the first stitch, and bring the needle back up through the fabric about ¼ inch (½ centimeter) from the end of the second stitch, then repeat steps 3–4.

# APPENDIX SIX:

# Quilting and Binding

Quilting is the result of sewing a top and bottom fabric together, usually with some kind of wadding in between. Before you stitch everything together, your pattern of sewn fabric blocks is just patchwork.

Depending on the size of your quilt, to quilt everything together can be a little fiddly, but it is fairly easy to do. There are several easy quilting stitching designs, including:

❑ "In the ditch" where you sew along or next to the seams of your fabric blocks, which hides the quilting stitch a little and makes the blocks really stand out. Check the Suit of Hearts project on page 97 to see this style of quilting.

❑ Straight lines, where you ignore the shape of your blocks and sew straight lines from edge to edge. These can be from top to bottom and side to side, making a grid pattern of quilting stitches, or diagonally both ways to create a diamond pattern. The Scrappy Quilt project on page 94 has a single diagonal quilting stitch.

❑ You can also try more tricky designs such as circles, spirals, wobbly random lines, or anything you like. You can do some test quilting on a small scrap fabric quilt sandwich to see each effect.

The more complicated the design, the harder it is going to be on a home sewing machine, so if this is one of your first quilts, I suggest trying a simple stitch like stitching in the ditch or straight lines.

And a quick note about wadding for the middle of the quilt—I usually use basic wool blankets from charity stores. I try to avoid anything with a pattern in the fabric itself, like cotton hospital style blankets, as the texture of the pattern can sometimes show through thinner cotton quilt tops.

For the backing of the quilt, I usually use a sheet or table cloth from a charity store. Sometimes your fabric isn't big enough for your quilt, but that's no problem. You can always patchwork together several fabrics to get it to the right size. For example, this is the back of the Suit of Hearts quilt. I wanted to use the red and black printed fabric, which was a skirt I'd bought from a secondhand store that I think was originally a table cloth. But there wasn't enough of it, so I added thick banding created from a vintage sheet. If you look carefully you'll see two heart blocks on the fabric too. This was to mend two rips in the red fabric. It's the same block as the front of the quilt, but a little smaller. Visible mending isn't just for clothes!

# Quilting

## DIRECTIONS

*Quilt top*

*Wadding/blanket*

*Backing fabric*

*Pins (safety pins for preference, straight pins can also be used)*

1. Lay your newly finished quilt top right side down on your ironing board and press the seams flat. It's usually a good idea to try to iron the seams in opposite directions; lay one row to the right and lay the next row to the left, this helps the quilt be less lumpy once it's finished. But sometimes that's a bit too difficult due to sewing or other factors, so just do your best.

2. Find a sizable and clean floor space clear of furniture, curious pets, and children. I use the kitchen floor, swept clean first.

3. Lay out your backing fabric, which should be a couple of inches (10 centimeters or more) bigger than your quilt top, right side to the floor.

4. On top of your backing fabric, lay your wadding/blanket. The wadding should also be a couple of inches (10 centimeters or more) bigger than your quilt top.

5. Lastly, lay out your quilt top. Try to center it in the middle of the other layers.

6. Next, you need to pin everything together in your newly created "quilt sandwich." Usually this is done using safety pins. You can get special quilting safety pins which have a bend in them to make piercing through the quilt sandwich easier, but these aren't totally necessary. You can also use straight pins, just be careful of the sharp points in the next few steps! I like to start in the middle of the quilt and pin every 12 inches (30 centimeters) or so in every direction. I've done them closer together for the example quilt because it's much smaller than a regular sized quilt. (There are also a couple of lines of stitching already in the photo. That's because I forgot to photograph the pinning stage and only realized after I started stitching. So just ignore those sneaky stitching lines for now.) Pin in the blocks, making sure not to pin over the seams where you're planning to sew. Try to ensure your quilt sandwich is as flat as possible, wrinkles are just going to trip you up.

7. Now it's time to get quilting! You can choose a thread color to either blend in or stand out from your quilt colors, and you can also have a different color in the bobbin, again to blend in or stand out from your backing fabric. I always like to choose a contrasting thread.

8. When stitching, I like to start in the middle and work outwards. This helps secure the quilt sandwich and stops the wadding from moving around inside as you go. To stitch in the ditch, roll half your quilt up lengthways to make it easier to feed through the sewing machine, and sew a straight line along the edge of the block closest to the center of your quilt to the bottom edge. Then go back to the middle and sew a straight line from the center point to the top edge. You might need to readjust the quilt a couple of times while sewing a row to make sure the weight of it isn't pulling at the fabric as it's running through the machine.

9. Make sure to run off either edge of the quilt top when you're stitching. You also don't need to backstitch the start and end of each row as the stitching will be captured with the binding so it can't unravel.

10. Now roll your quilt halfway widthways, and repeat the sewing from the center to the outer edge. This divides your quilt into four and helps hold the wadding and backing fabric in place as you continue quilting. There might be the occasional wobbly seams, embrace them. They're signatures of the uniqueness of your awesome handmade quilt. This is the point when I took the above photo.

11. Sometimes your blocks won't quite match up, but there's no need to worry. Your quilting seam can drift left or right to accommodate this and to head back into the ditch. Think about it a quilting version of "the line of best fit."

12. Now roll the quilt halfway up lengthways again, and continue stitching in the ditch from the middle seam to the edge until the quarter is quilted, then repeat for the other quarters until the whole quilt is stitched. A quick note—the more stitching lines, the stiffer the quilt will be, so I tend not to do too many stitching lines. That way my quilts are nice and floppy and good to snuggle under.

## BINDING

If you're binding a hexie quilt, you'll need to cut through every second hexie around the edge to form a nice straight line to bind.

### WHAT YOU'LL NEED

*Binding fabric
(amount below)*

### DIRECTIONS

1. First, trim any excess wadding and backing fabric away so your quilt edges all align.

2. To find out how much binding you need, measure the perimeter of your quilt and add 9 inches (23 centimeters) to account for seams and corners.

3. Measure the length of your binding fabric. You'll be cutting 3-inch wide strips (7½ centimeters) to create the binding, but how many strips will depend on your final number from step 2. Length of perimeter plus an extra 9 inches (23 centimeters)=X. X divided by the width of the binding fabric=how many strips you'll need to cut. It sounds a little complicated, but it's pretty simple when you get the hang of it. For example, my Suit of Hearts quilt perimeter is 166 inches (421 centimeters), so adding the extra 9 inches (23 centimeters) for seams and corners comes out to a total of 175 inches (444 centimeters). My binding fabric was 45 inches (114 centimeters) wide, so I divided 175 inches (444 centimeters) by 45 inches (114 centimeters) to find out how many strips I'd need to cut from the binding fabric. This number ends up being 3.888888888, so I rounded that figure up to 4. This means I cut 4 binding strips the length of my binding fabric by 3 inches (7½ centimeters) wide.

4. To sew the binding together into one long strip, place two strips with their right sides together at a 90 degree angle. You'll be sewing diagonally across this, which spreads the seam across the binding strip, rather than doing a straight seam, which would bulk out the binding at that point. You can draw a line to follow or just wing it.

5. Sew diagonally together corner to corner.

6. Open up the binding to make sure that you've sewn it correctly. The binding should continue in one long strip with the right sides of the fabric both facing out.

7. Once you're sure you have sewn it correctly (which took me a couple of times to get right when I started), cut the excess off.

8. Continue joining your binding strips together.

9. Iron seams open, again to distribute the bulkiness of the fabric.

10. Now fold your binding strip in half lengthways with the wrong sides together and the right sides out and iron flat. And your binding strip is done!

## STITCHING THE BINDING STRIP TO THE QUILT

11. Starting in the middle of one side of your quilt, and leaving a 6-inch (15 centimeters) "tail" on the binding, run your binding around the whole quilt to make sure you don't have any seams landing on the corners. If you do, move the starting place up or down a few inches or centimeters to avoid the seams at the corners.

12. Place the binding at the back of the quilt with the raw open edges of the binding against the edge of the quilt. I don't generally pin binding, but feel free to do so if you prefer.

13. Stitch the binding in place, stitching ¼ inch (6 mm) from the edge.

14. When approaching a corner, stop sewing ¼ inch (6 mm) from the edge of the quilt (mark it beforehand with a pin if you need to). Turn your quilt 45 degrees and sew diagonally up to the edge of the tip.

15. Spin the quilt so the edge you've just sewn is now at the top.

16. Now to make your corner. Firstly, fold the unsewn tail of the binding straight up, so its raw edge is parallel with the next side of the quilt to be bound.

17. Fold the binding strip back down parallel with the unbound side of the quilt, running the raw edge along the next side of the quilt and creating a tuck of fabric at the corner.

18. Sew the binding down the next side of the quilt, starting ¼ inch (6 mm) away from the top edge and making sure you don't sew the folded tuck of fabric. Repeat this process for all four corners.

19. When you get near the end, stop 6 inches (15 centimeters) away from the starting edge of the binding so there is now a 12-inch (30 centimeters) gap in stitching.

20. To join the ends of the binding, make sure your binding overlaps itself by 3 inches (7½ centimeters) (trim away any excess) and pin the tails right sides together in a right angle.

21. To check you're sewing the correct angle, unfold the pinned binding. Does your angle make a continuous binding or is it tangled? If so, unpin and try again.

22. While checking that your angle is right, check also to see that the binding is the right length. If it's too long for the quilt, adjust the join tighter until it lays flat.

23. Once you have the right angle, sew from corner to corner.

24. Lay the quilt flat to check the length and angle is right before trimming the corners.

25. Continue sewing the raw edge of the binding to the quilt.

26. Now flip the quilt over so that the front of the quilt is facing up.

27. Pull the folded edge of the binding over the raw edge of the quilt to cover the line of stitching and pin down.

28. Stitch along the binding ¼ inch (6 mm) from the folded edge of the binding. If the quilt is getting a little bulky under the binding, run your finger between the quilt and binding to smooth down and continue stitching.

29. When you get near the corner, stitch to 2 inches (5 centimeters) away from the edge, then stop.

30. Fold the corner into a neat miter and stitch slowly towards it, making sure it feeds smoothly under the sewing machine foot.

31. Stitch a few stitches into the folded corner, then with your needle still in the fabric, turn the quilt 45 degrees and sew down the next side.

32. Continue sewing around the rest of the quilt, following steps 29 to 30 for each corner.

# APPENDIX SEVEN:

# Patterns

Due to the limited dimensions of this book, the following patterns appear smaller than recommended in my projects: Guerrilla Kindness Cupcake, The (Secret) Toy Society Guerrilla Kindness Bottle, Protest Banner letters, Pennants History Hexie Pattern, and Tshirt stencil. To access and trace the full size patterns please visit my website at http://sayraphimlothian.com/patterns to download them for free.

Use the access code GKPatterns.

cake base

icing top

cake

icing side

ABCDEFGHIJK
LMNOPQRSTU
VWXYZ

Body
cut 2
MF

CF - contrasting fabric    W - white    ------- snip line
MF - main fabric           B - black

Nose
cut 1 B

Belly
cut 1
CF

Leg
cut 4
MF

Arm
cut 4
MF

Eye
outside
cut 2
W

Muzzle
cut 1
CF

Pointed
ear
cut 2 MF
2 CF

Rounded
ear
cut 2 MF
2 CF

Eye
inside
cut 2
B

Tail
cut 2
MF

Label
cut 1

Bottle
cut 4

Base
cut 1

| | |
|---|---|
| 30 | |
| | 29 |
| 28 | |
| | 27 |
| 26 | |
| | 25 |
| short skirt/ dress/shorts 24 | |
| legs | 23 |
| 22 | |
| | 21 |
| 20 | |
| | 19 |
| 18 | |
| knee lenth skirt/ dress/shorts | 17 |
| legs 16 | |
| | 15 |
| 14 | |
| | 13 |
| 12 | |
| | 11 |
| 10 | |
| | 9 |
| long pants 8 | |
| feet | 7 |
| 6 | |
| | 5 |
| 4 | |
| | 3 |
| 2 | |
| | 1 |

# PATTERN PROTEST DOLL-DRESS

cast off here for
long dress

cast off here for
mid length dress

cast off here for
short dress

suit jacket
neckline

34
32
30
28
26
24
22
20
18
16
14
12
10
8
6
4
2

35
33
31
29
27
25
23
21
19
17
15
13
11
9
7
5
3
1

# PATTERN PROTEST DOLL-ARM

t-shirt sleeves
arms

30
29
28
27
26
25
24
23
22
21
20
19
18
17
16
15
14
13
12
11
10
9
8
7
6
5
4
3
2
1

elbow length sleeves
arms

long sleeves
hands

PATTERN PROTEST DOLL-HEAD

hairline
face

20
18
16
14
12
10
8
6
4
2

21
19
17
15
13
11
9
7
5
3
1

# PATTERN BLANK GRID

Black
Lives
Matter

## CROSS STITCH ALPHABET

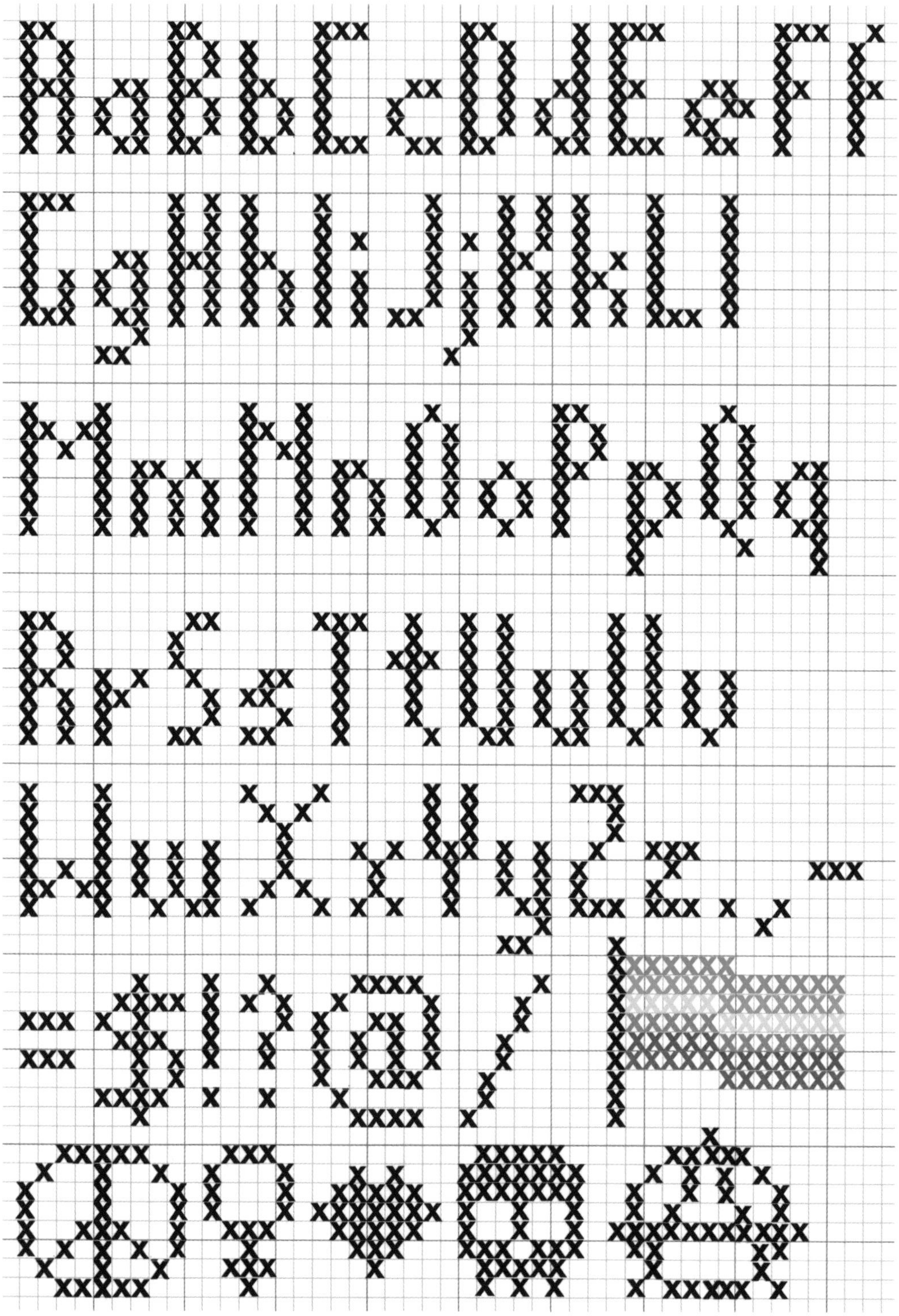

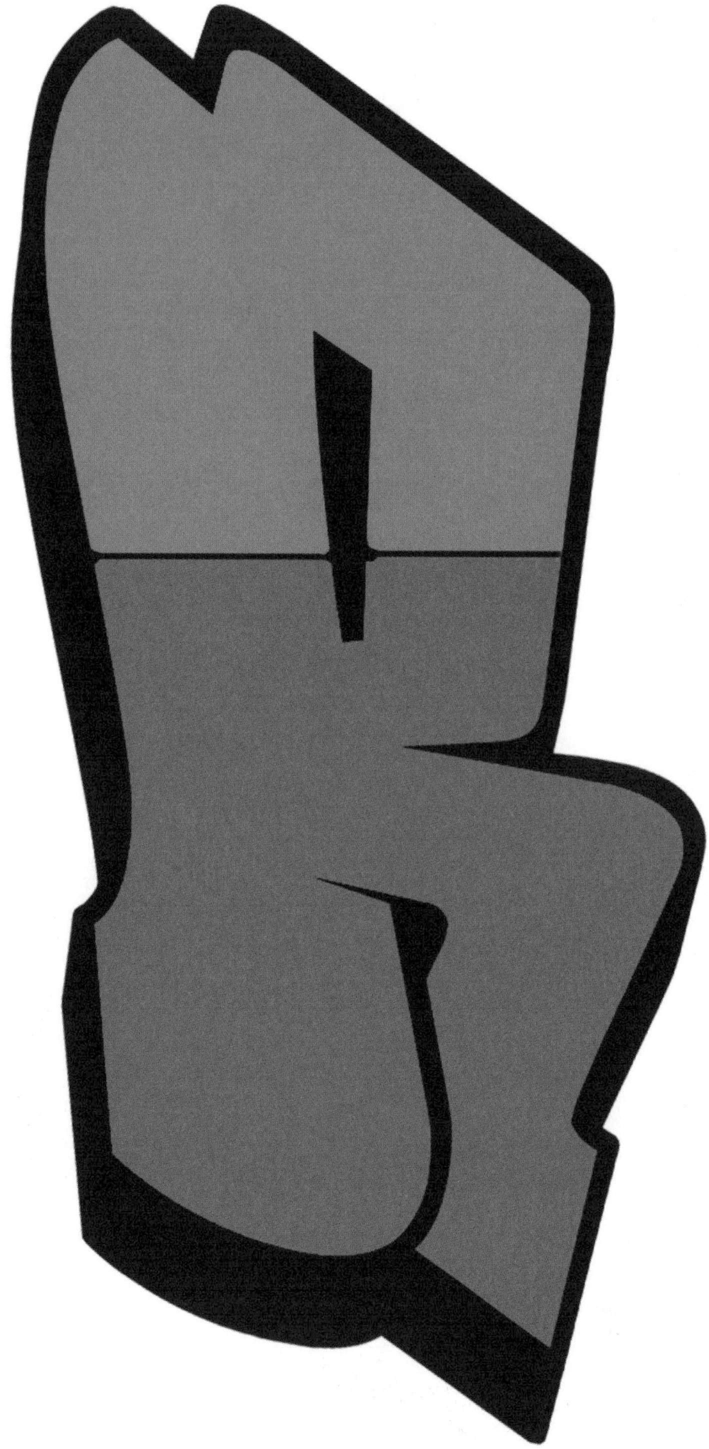

## PATTERN PATTERN PROTEST BANNER E

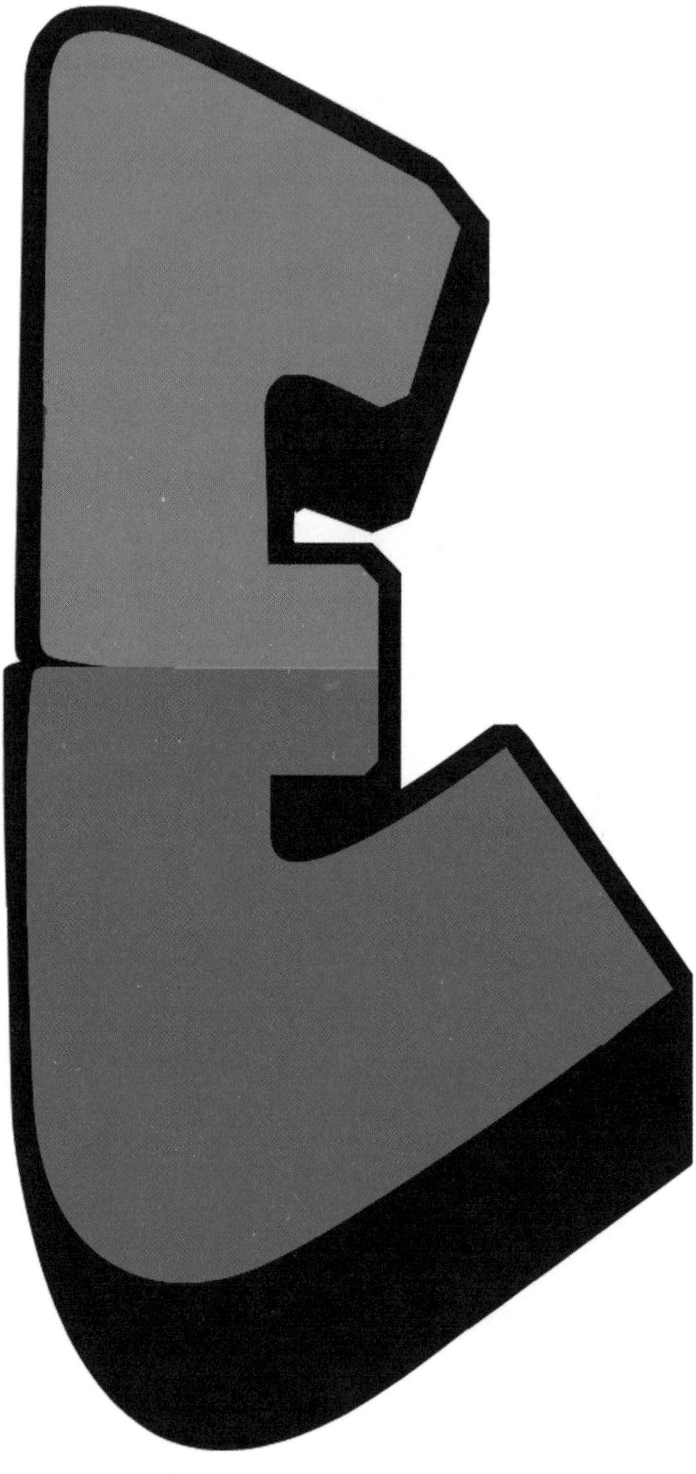

## PATTERN PATTERN PROTEST BANNER S

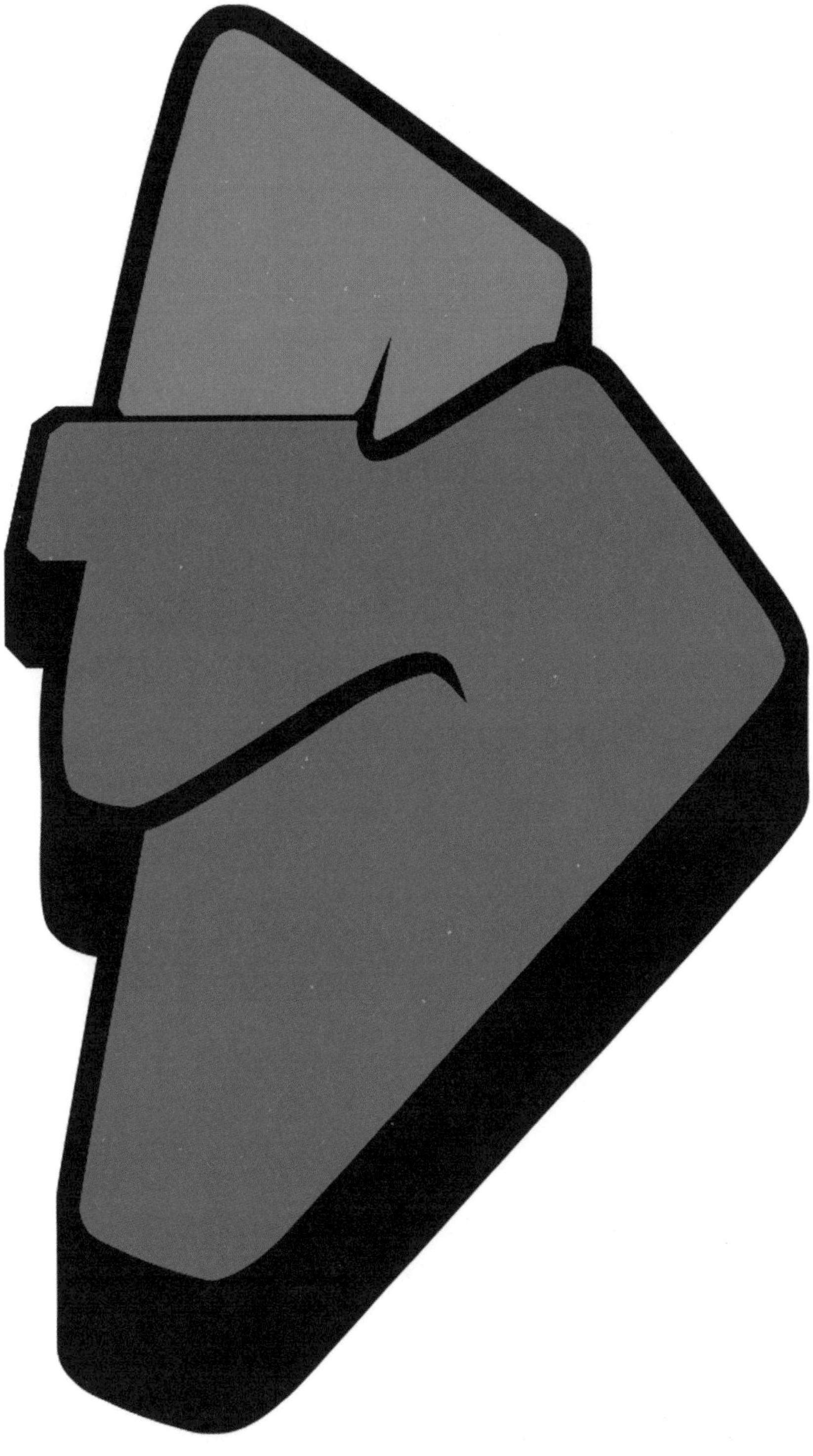

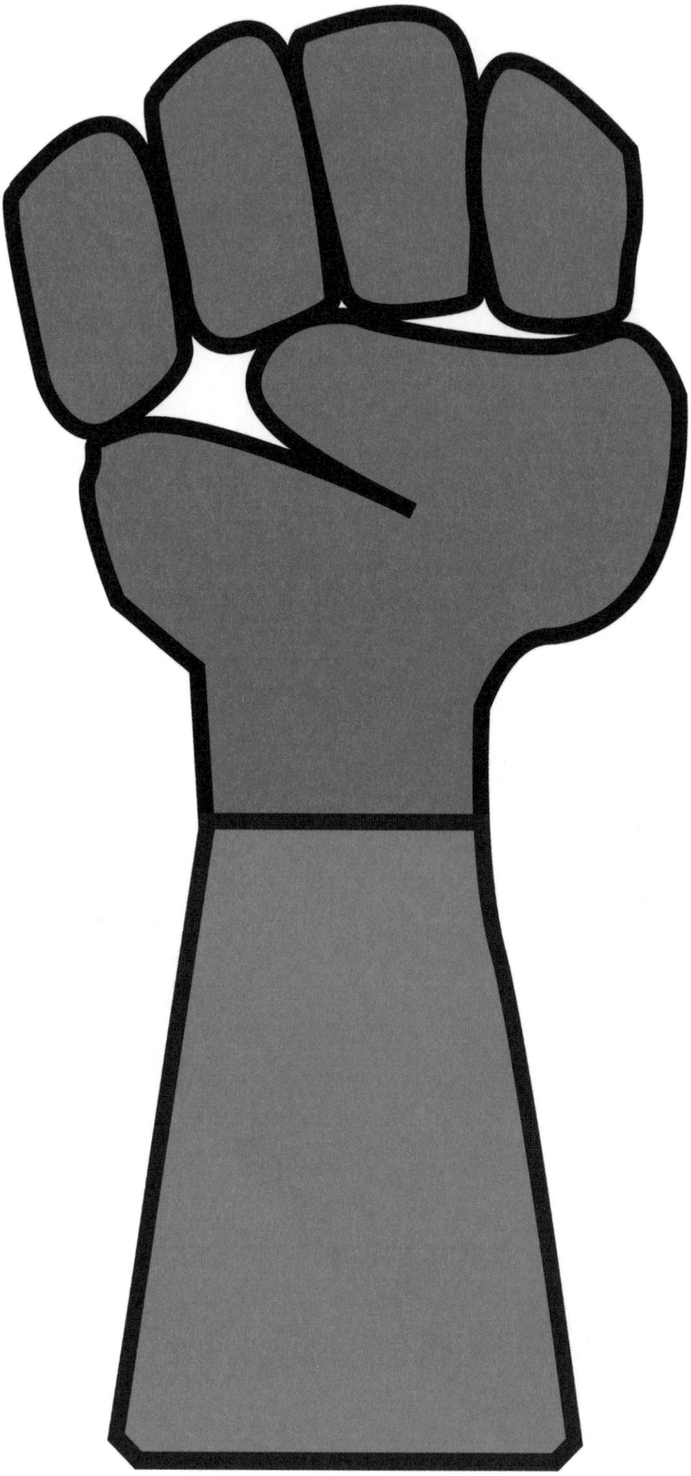

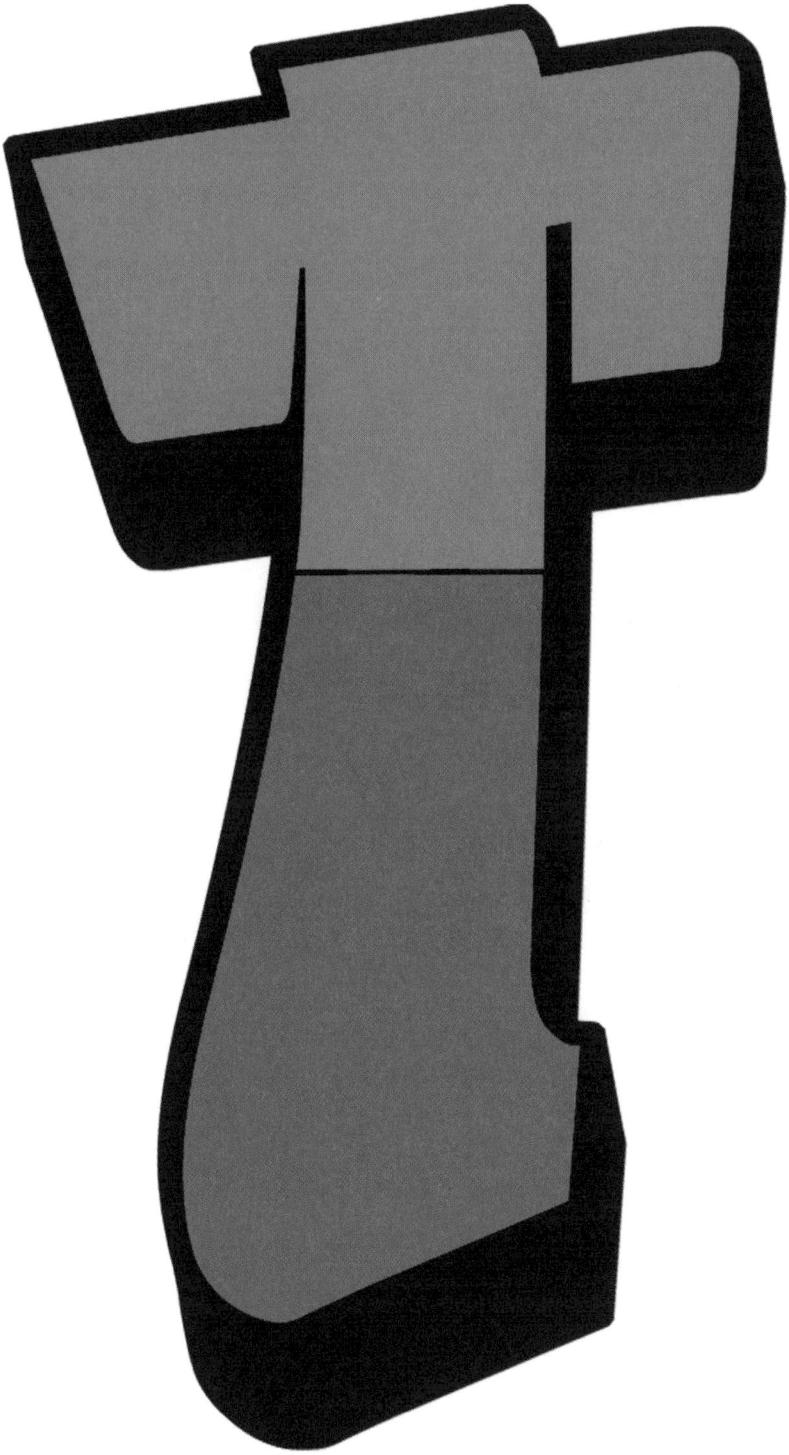

# DAMN RIGHT WE'RE ANGRY

PATTERN PENNANT 2

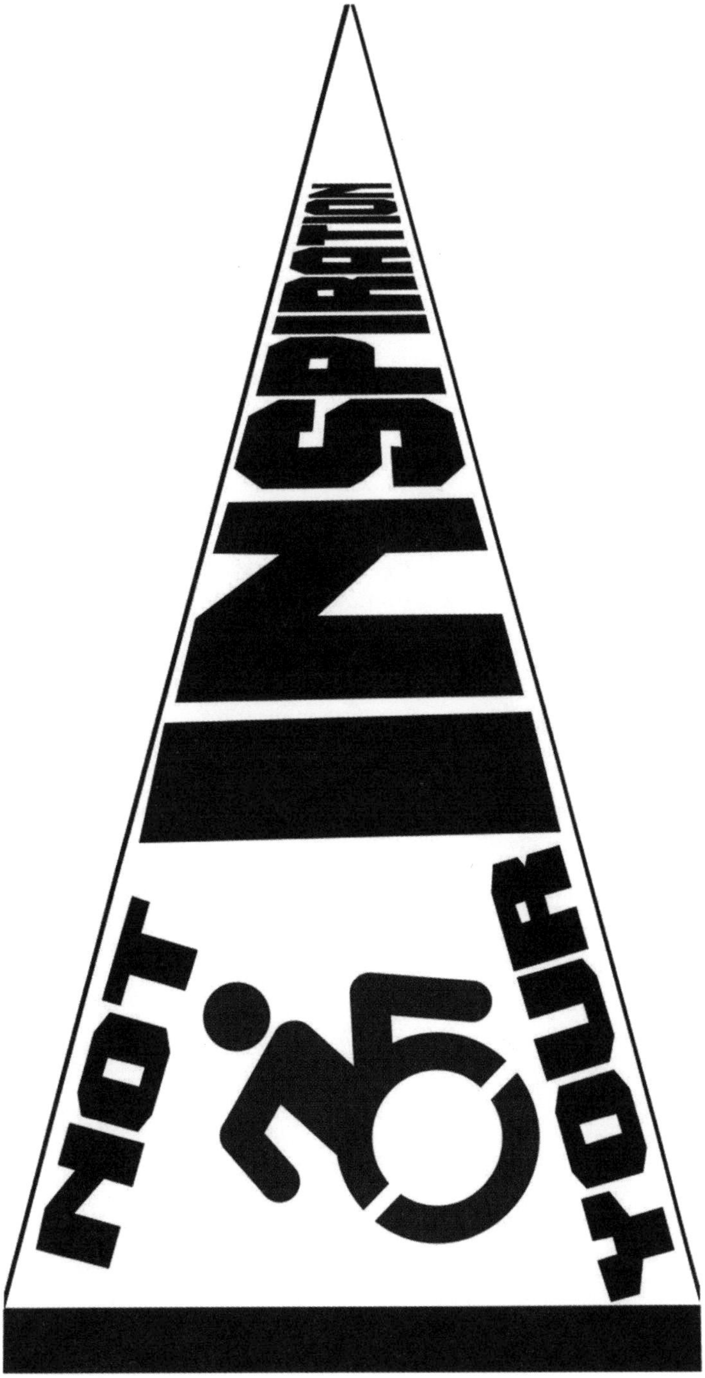

## PATTERN QUILTED PATCH

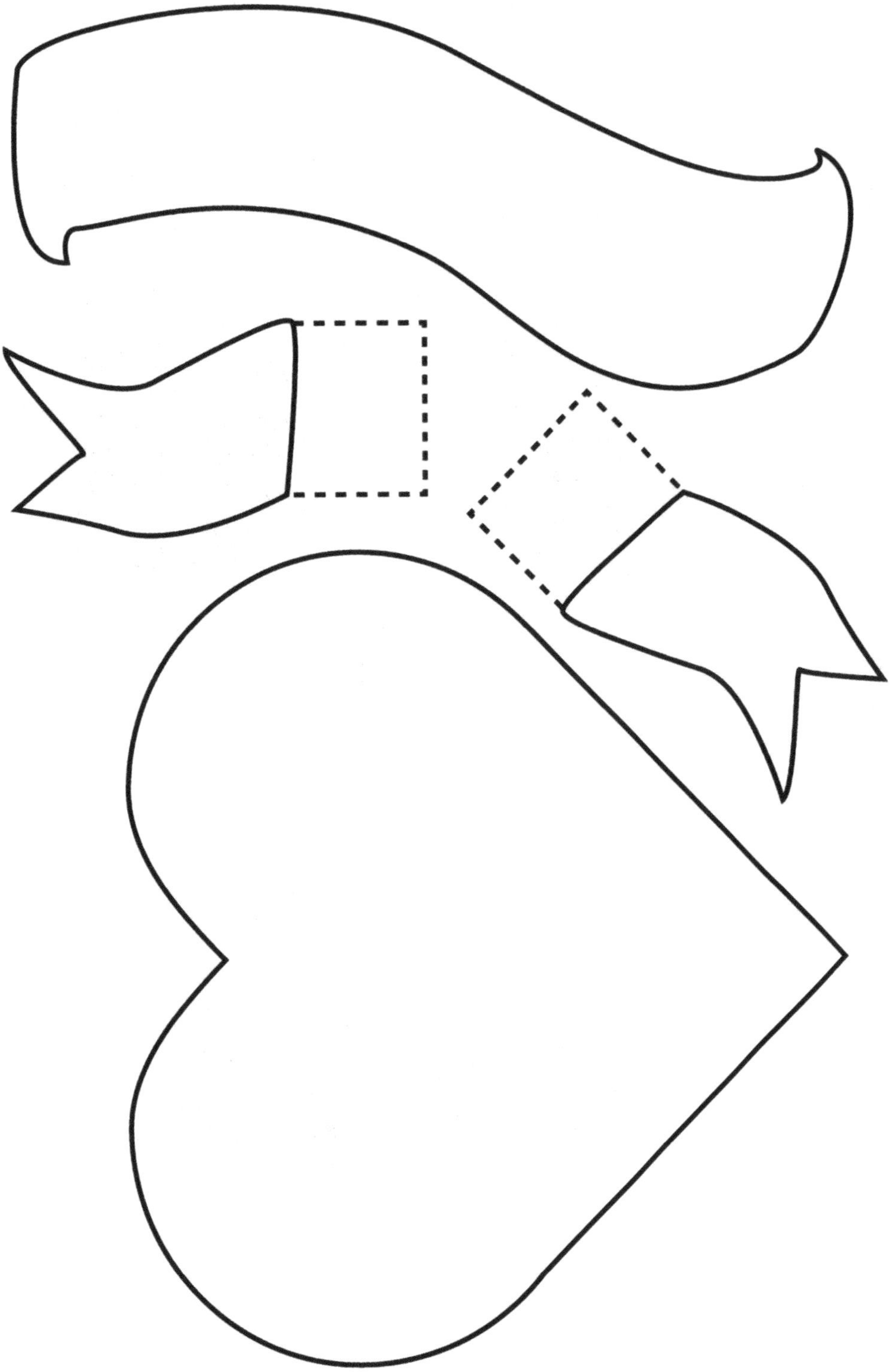

## PATTERN KNITTED SKULL

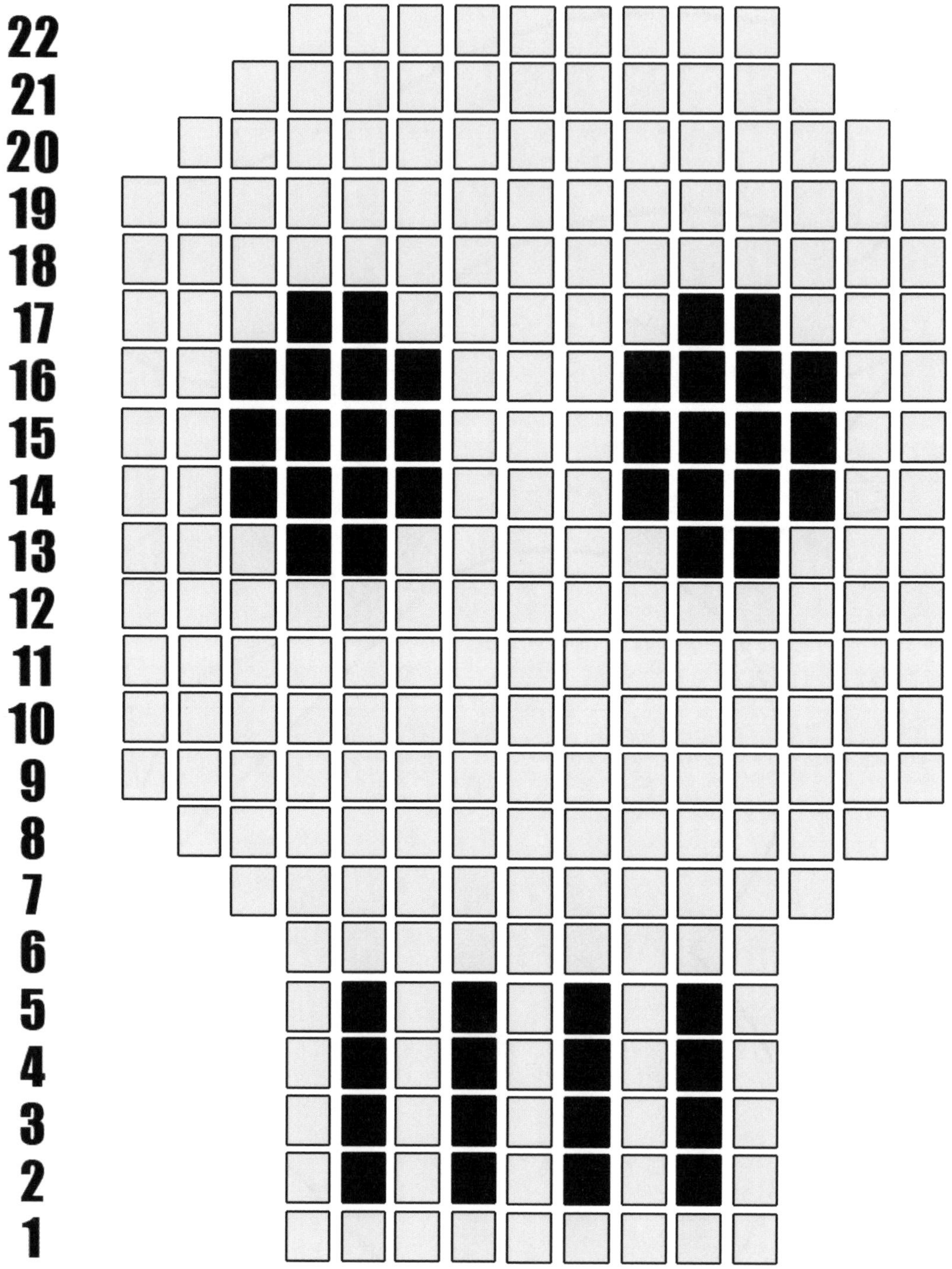

# RIOTS NOT DIETS

CRipPLepUNK

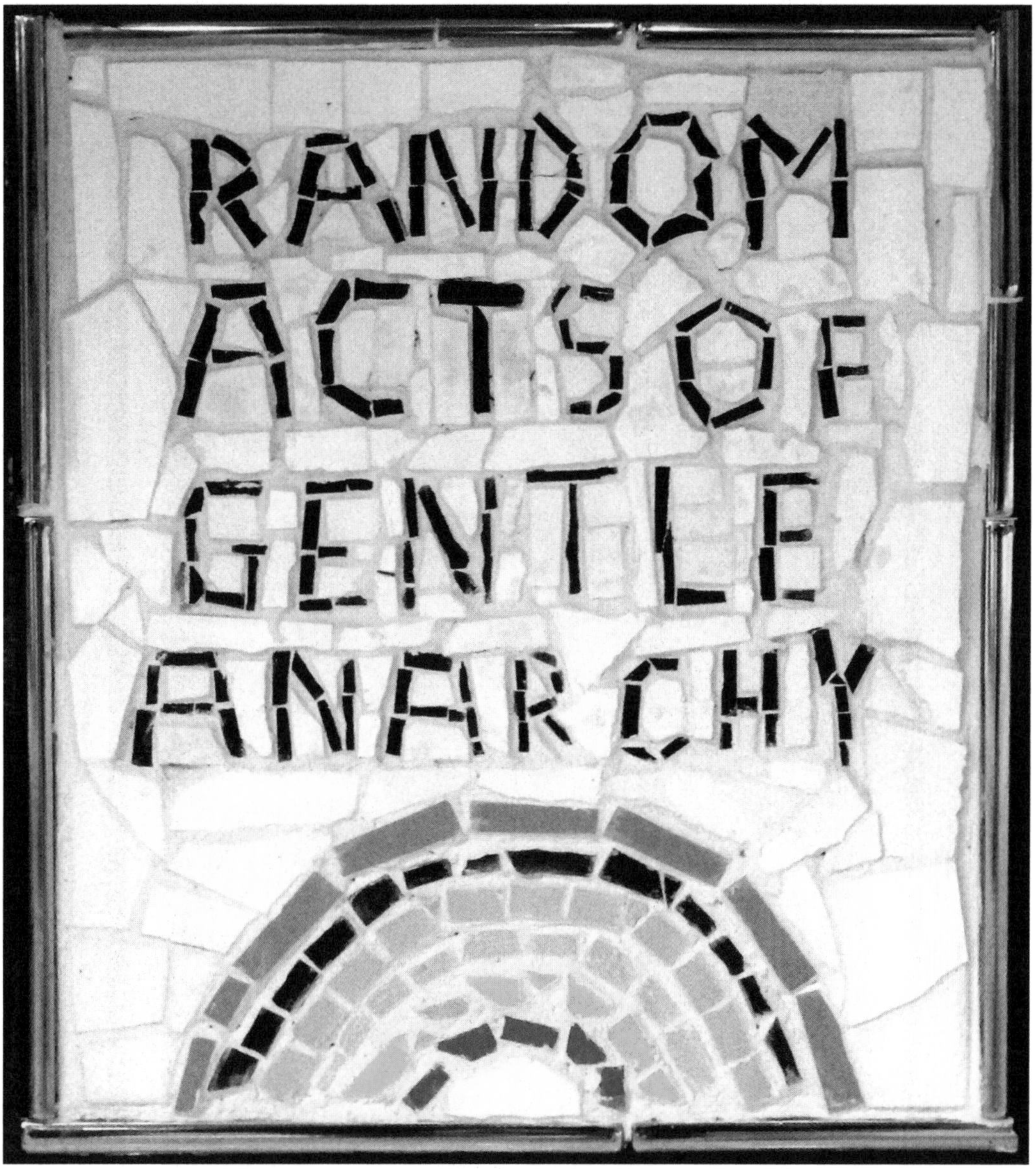
RANDOM
ACTS OF
GENTLE
ANARCHY

COMMIT NO NUISANCE

Thanks boys,
I've got this one...

# About the Author

I am a public artist, craftivist, academic, and mischief maker. I acknowledge my privileges include being white, middle-class, able-bodied, and postgraduate educated. I was born in Wurundjeri country, raised in Ngunnawal country, educated in Dja Dja Wurrung and Taungurung country, and now live back in Wurundjeri country.

My mother, Cristine, taught me activism. She was and is a staunch feminist, so growing up, my younger sister and I went on lots of marches with her—women's lib, reclaim the night, and peace marches and others. We were tiny and cute, so people would give us banners to wave when we hadn't made our own. We'd get to shout stuff, and it was always great fun. My mother was instrumental in setting up the first women's neighborhood house in Canberra, and on Friday nights we'd get pizza and chips and take them to the women's house, where they would debate issues for hours. We'd play games and eventually fall asleep listening to their discussions. She was a single mother, a teacher, and a proud union member all her working life. I remember going to stop work meetings with her. We'd be in a hall full of teachers, entertaining ourselves at the back with a washing basket of toys while they worked hard to make the teachers' lot better.

Because she was a teacher, she had access to her school's badge making machine, and she'd bring it home some weekends for us all to make activist badges. My favorite causes back then were feminism, kids' rights, and animal rights, so I made a lot of those badges. Some I kept, but some I gave away to friends at school.

Mum taught us the importance of being strong and independent women from an early age. At the same time, my grandmother, Marjory Jane, taught me craft and generosity. She was retired and spent all year knitting and sewing dolls with her local Country Women's Association. She was at various times president, treasurer, or secretary of her local chapter. The other ladies would make clothes, knit scarves, or make preserves, and at the end of the year, they'd set up a stall at their local shopping mall to sell what they'd made and donate all the proceeds to charity. Then in January, she'd start making all over again for the next year. I remember whenever I went to her house, I'd always beg her to open the cupboard where she kept all the finished dolls and show me what she'd made. That cupboard was a magical, colorful space stuffed with handmade treasures.

Nan had an enormous stash. People knew that she was on a pension and that she spent the year making things for charity, so they'd donate heaps of material, yarn, stuffing, and thread. She kept it all in her garage sorted according to color. There was generosity in every stage of these toys' creation, and occasionally she'd make a special one for us. My favorite toys from childhood were the two dolls she made me when I was about three. I still have them.

She taught me to knit when I was young, and I remember watching in awe as she knitted without looking while watching television. When I tried it, I dropped more stitches than I managed. Even when I was a young adult, she was still teaching me clever crafting tricks and helping me with projects. When she was older, Nan had dementia and was living in a high care home, but even then, she was still crafting. After she passed away, a young nurse told us that in the last few weeks of my grandmother's life, Nan had taught her how to knit a scarf, which was a skill she'd treasure forever.

I am proud to come from a family of activist and creative women.

Now I work as a public artist who utilizes as many crafts as I can turn my hand to. I'm interested in activism and creative resistance around the world, and my body of work revolves around kindness as a form of rebellion, craft as a form of subversion, and playfulness in public to overturn expected behaviors. I'm inspired by street art, craft history, and rebelliousness in almost all its forms.

**See more of my work on social media:**

Instagram and twitter: @sayraphim
Facebook: www.facebook.com/sayraphimlothian
YouTube: www.youtube.com/c/monsterthinks
Website: www.sayraphimlothian.com